J. McGovern

Choices

D0591851

Choices

Ethics and the Christian

David Brown

Basil Blackwell

© David Brown 1983

First published 1983
Reprinted 1983
Basil Blackwell Publisher Limited
108 Cowley Road, Oxford OX4 1JF, England

All rights reserved. No part of this publication may be reproduced, stored in a retrieval system, or transmitted, in any form or by any means, electronic, mechanical, photocopying, recording or otherwise, without the prior permission of the publisher.

Except in the United States of America, this book is sold subject to the condition that it shall not, by way or trade or otherwise, be lent, re-sold, hired out, or otherwise circulated without the publisher's prior consent in any form of binding or cover other than that in which it is published and without a similar condition including this condition being imposed on the subsequent purchaser.

British Library Cataloguing in Publication Data

Brown, David
   Choices—(Faith and the future)
   1. Christian ethics
   I. Title   II. Series
   241   BJ1251

   ISBN 0-631-13182-5
   ISBN 0-631-13222-8 Pbk

Typeset by Cambrian Typesetters,
Farnborough, Hants
Printed in Great Britain by
T. J. Press Ltd, Padstow

Contents

BJ
1251
. B76
1983

Foreword

This book is one of a series whose writers consider some important aspects of Christianity in the contemporary scene and in so doing draw inspiration from the Catholic revival in the Anglican Communion which began in Oxford one hundred and fifty years ago. This revival — with its thinkers, pastors, prophets, social reformers and not a few who have been held to be saints — has experienced changes in the understanding of the Christian faith since the time of the Tractarians and has none the less borne witness to themes which are deep and unchanging. Among these are the call to holiness, the communion of saints, the priesthood of the Church and its ministers and a sacramental religion, both otherworldly and with revolutionary claims upon man's social life.

I am myself convinced that the renewal of the Church for today and tomorrow needs a deep recovery of these themes of Catholic tradition and a vision of their contemporary application. The books of this series are designed towards this end, and I am sure that readers will be grateful for the help they give. Many are thirsty but 'the well is deep'.

+ Michael Ramsey

Preface

Most introductions to Christian ethics are either highly general or concerned with only one or two specific themes. Also, they often give the impression of presenting a particular author's opinions, and no more. I have tried to avoid these faults, and to write an introduction to Christian ethics that both argues for certain general principles (the first two chapters) and discusses a large number of specific ethical issues (the remaining four chapters). In addition, I give some indication of the range of past and present views on the subject. Even so, limitations of space have prevented discussion of many important issues, e.g. the Third World.

In chapter 2, writings of the Oxford Movement are used to illustrate the general principles. But, as I attempt to show, there is no reason why they should appeal only to those who label themselves Roman Catholic or Anglo-Catholic. One can be a Catholic in ethics without necessarily abandoning one's overall doctrinal position.

Special attention is given to the role of argument. In chapter 2 I have attempted to justify the idea of a continuing core in Catholic ethics. At the same time, when dealing with specific issues, I have explained why some past views have come under attack or been abandoned. More importantly, the reasons for present positions are carefully scrutinized.

Suggestions for further reading are to be found at the end of each chapter, as well as in the body of the text; almost all these books are in print and easily accessible. Details of the books quoted or mentioned in the text are provided in a list of references at the end of the book. Bible quotations are mostly from the Authorized Version.

In a few, indicated, instances I have used the New English Bible translation.

I am very grateful to Perry Butler, F. W. Dillistone, Michael and Julia Ipgrave, and David Nicholls (the editor of the series), for reading and commenting on a previous draft, and for the care they took to ensure that the book would be readily intelligible to the general reader. I am also grateful to Professor Ernest Nicholson who acted as Chaplain of Oriel during the term in which it was completed.

David Brown

1 The Secular Challenge
Contemporary Secular Ethics and the Inadequate Christian Response

It is a truism that we live in a pluralistic culture. This is reflected not merely in the variety of faiths and non-faiths to be found in our midst, but also in the Church itself. No longer can one be certain of a person's doctrinal convictions simply by discovering his or her denominational label. Some Presbyterians and Methodists are more Catholic in their approach than the average Anglican; some Roman Catholics more Protestant in their assumptions than the typical Anglo-Catholic.

But it is in the field of ethics that the most bewildering variety exists. On almost every issue one finds practising Christians ranged on both sides, whether it be sexual ethics, abortion, nuclear warfare or whatever. Even apartheid is no exception, since one cannot deny the obvious sincerity of many members of the Dutch Reformed Church in South Africa. Nor is terrorism. Some members of the Provisional IRA are undoubtedly devout Catholics, even daily communicants, as, for instance, the Price sisters. Little wonder then that Christians are often confused about what they ought to say on particular ethical issues. More worrying, when they do say something, the reasons they give for their opinions are often woefully inadequate, a point that applies as much to the professional theologian as to the educated layman. Paul Ramsey, the distinguished American ethicist, has recently described the current situation in Christian ethics as 'a virtual wasteland' for this very reason. In what follows, therefore, we shall concentrate primarily upon the *reasons* on which Christian ethical pronouncements should be based. But first I shall present some

1

alternative options, both secular and Christian, with which the Catholic answer should be contrasted.

SECULAR ALTERNATIVES: UTILITARIANISM AND MARXISM

A surprisingly large percentage of our contemporaries would reject the notion of ethics altogether and claim that all anyone ever does, or can do, is to pursue their own interest — a position known as psychological egoism. But that all this amounts to is a cynical attempt at self-justification is shown clearly by the undoubted cases of heroic concern for others that have occurred. Even if the egoist were to claim that all instances of altruism involving Christians were motivated by a selfish desire to get to heaven, examples of such behaviour by non-believers could easily be adduced.

The serious alternatives to Christianity thus lie elsewhere. Two in particular must be singled out: Utilitarianism and Marxism. The reason for this is that, arguably, they are at present the two most popularly canvassed approaches to ethics, one representing the main stream of contemporary Western liberal thought, the other its main radical alternative. Yet, if one stands outside both, one is immediately struck more by their similarities than by their differences. First, both are nineteenth-century creations. Marx died in 1883 and the two people who first seriously developed Utilitarianism as an ethical system are Jeremy Bentham, who died in 1832, and his more famous successor, John Stuart Mill, who died in 1873. Secondly, both were innovating systems concerned to advocate change. Marx was reacting against the conservatism of the German philosopher, Hegel, while Bentham and Mill were both actively involved with penal and legal reforms. Also both are really 'umbrella' terms, in the sense that widely diverging views can be found sheltering under the same label with little in common apart from the original source of inspiration. Indeed, even the question of tolerance, which is often seen as the main difference between the two, cannot be regarded as an absolute difference. Witness the

2

greater acceptance of tolerance in the Euro-Communism of Italy and Spain on the one hand, and on the other the common contention that there is no necessary theoretical incompatibility between Utilitarianism and the practice of slavery. Much the same could be said concerning the debate about whether the proposed change should be gradual or revolutionary. Advocates of both positions can now be drawn from either camp.

All these points of similarity, however, pale into insignificance when compared with their main point of contact, namely their 'consequentialist' framework — the view that moral action is to be judged solely in terms of its overall consequences. As this is a point of some importance for what follows, it is worth spending a little time over. The Utilitarian slogan, 'the greatest happiness of the greatest number', has been interpreted in many different ways. For instance, it has sometimes been taken as a demand simply to produce the maximum amount of pleasure, irrespective of how many or how few people it is distributed amongst, while other advocates would insist that the most important factor to be taken into account is its spread. Both are versions of what is known as Act Utilitarianism. Rule Utilitarianism interprets the slogan as justification for a system of rules which in general are to be obeyed, except in conflict situations where arbitration is necessary by direct appeal to the maximization of pleasure or utility. But what these and other variants all share in common is the basic conviction that the morality of action is to be judged by its results or consequences.

The same assumption underlies Marxism, though in this case there is no simple, summing-up slogan. The absence of such a slogan can in part be explained by Marx's commitment to the view that there is an inevitability about the historical process. For ethics then becomes a matter of one's endorsement of this process, and it is not of much significance whether one justifies one's conduct in terms of the ultimate end, the 'withering away of the state', or the intermediate steps towards that end, such as 'the heightening of the consciousness of the masses' that must precede

3

the revolution, or 'the dictatorship of the proletariat' that will immediately follow it. Part of the explanation may also lie in the vagueness of the ultimate ideal, in which the dictatorship of the proletariat, the need for the apparatus of the state, disappears with the perfect reconciliation of everyone's interests. But, even if one cannot point to a single criterion of action in Marxism, its general conse-quantialist thrust cannot be in doubt. For all one needs to do in order to justify one's action is to show that its net result is some contribution towards the advancement of this historical process, even if it is only a very intermediate stage.

That human happiness and the reconciliation of interests are laudable ideals, no one would deny. Rather, the question is, at what price is their realization to be bought? As these first two chapters unfold, we shall gradually see that a very heavy price has been paid. For the moment, however, it will suffice to draw attention to one issue only, the question of whether the end can be allowed to justify the means. Twice in the Epistle to the Romans (3:8 and 6:1) St Paul raises the question whether one may do evil that good may come, and twice gives an emphatic, 'No'. Admittedly, the context is a rather specialized theological one, but there seems no reason to doubt that Paul would have endorsed the commonly made, wider application of the passage. At all events, as we shall see, the Christian ethical tradition can offer very good grounds for giving such an emphatic, 'No'. But at this stage of our discussion let the reader simply test his intuitions against the following cases.

On the Marxist side, the best-known discussion of the relation between means and ends is probably the celebrated debate between Leon Trotsky and the American philosopher John Dewey that took place in 1938. Trotsky, considering what means might legitimately be employed in the class struggle against capitalism and in particular whether lying, frame-up, betrayal and murder could ever be justified, answered that 'permissible and obligatory are those and only those means . . . which unite the revolutionary proletariat'. Although he went on to point out

4

that 'precisely from this it flows that not all means are permissible', the point to be noted is that his exclusion of certain means is pragmatic, not moral, because as a matter of fact they will in certain instances fail to realize the objectives in question. Nor is this pragmatic approach, with no conduct whatsoever ruled out in advance, unique to Trotsky. It emerges just as clearly in the attitude of Engels, Marx's collaborator, to Irish terrorism. Despite having a Fenian as a common-law wife, Lizzy Burns, he condemned Irish terrorist acts, not on grounds of morality but rather because they were counter-productive. The Clerkenwell explosion, for instance, had simply produced blind rage in British public opinion. Lenin equally refused to exclude any means from consideration. Indeed, he called Plekanov's rejection of terror 'philistine', a curious use of the word, to say the least.

Utilitarianism shows more reticence in revealing its hand in this matter, but Bentham certainly thought that there were occasions when the use of torture would be justified. In general, however, the usual Utilitarian strategy is either to amend the system and then argue that by so doing such problem cases will not arise — Rule Utilitarianism is one such attempt — or to maintain, as in Professor Hare's recent book *Moral Thinking*, that in fact conflict situations between our ordinary moral intuitions and Utilitarianism seldom occur. Admittedly some of the counter-examples suggested have an air of unreality about them. But even with the punishment of an innocent man it is all too credible that a successful frame-up could be perpetrated and justified in terms of society's overall utilitarian advantage (e.g. the removal behind bars of a notorious trouble-maker). Indeed, if some minorities are to be believed, this has already happened on several occasions. Again, to give a more everyday example, we all make promises which in retrospect it makes no sense to keep if we average out the utility or happiness of everyone involved, including ourselves. Nonetheless, we feel we ought to keep them simply because we have put ourselves under an obligation to the person to whom the promise was made.

But, enough of this appeal to our intuitions. In order to see more clearly what is wrong with this type of approach to ethics, we turn now to a consideration of their Christian imitations.

CHRISTIAN IMITATIONS: SITUATION ETHICS AND LIBERATION THEOLOGY

Because Christianity is a missionary religion, convinced that it has the only adequate answer to man's problems, there is an inevitable temptation on the part of its adherents to suppose that any alternative that has intellectual or popular appeal must already be implicit within Christianity itself. The result is Christian Utilitarians and Christian Marxists, though the phenomenon is by no means so narrowly confined. The extent to which churchmen pronounce on ecological issues is, for example, surely to be explained more by the present popularity of the topic than by its moral importance, just as the absence of ecclesiastical comment on the barbaric conditions in some of our prisons can equally be explained by the antipathy this would arouse.

So far as Christian Utilitarianism is concerned, it is best known under the name of 'situation ethics' from its popularization in the book of the same name by the American ethicist, Joseph Fletcher. A major contributing factor to its popularity was the endorsement of the position by John Robinson in his best-seller *Honest to God*, where he described situation ethics as 'the only ethic for "man come of age" '. Fletcher's basic contention is that Christian ethics must escape from the two extremes of legalism and antinomianism (no rules), and instead adopt a middle course with love as the only standard and each situation assessed in terms of love and love alone. Superficially, this sounds very different from the secular norm, but in fact the same conduct is advocated, and at one point Fletcher admits that his whole strategy is utilitarian:

6

It becomes plain that as the love ethic searches seriously for a social policy it must form a coalition with utilitarianism. It takes over from Bentham and Mill the strategic principle of 'the greatest good of the greatest number'. Observe that this is a genuine coalition, even though it reshapes the 'good' of the utilitarians, replacing their pleasure principle with agape (love). In the coalition the hedonistic calculus becomes the agapeistic calculus, the greatest amount of neighbor welfare for the greatest number of neighbors possible. (*Situation Ethics,* p. 95)

If we now look at the way Fletcher applies this principle in practice, we shall soon see why it must be judged a complete perversion of the notion of love. He tells us, for instance, that, if a priest learns under the seal of the confessional that an innocent man is about to die for what is in fact the penitent's crime, he should have no hesitation in informing the authorities. But what he ignores with his agapeistic calculus is the special relationship which exists between priest and penitent. The penitent presumably trusts the priest. Indeed, the very fact that he chooses to go to confession at all must surely show some desire to mend his ways. If that is so, then the priest's first obligation, given this special relation of trust, must be to help the penitent make a proper contrition, even if he cannot secure this immediately by urging him to make his confession public (e.g. because of the penitent's terror of death or anxiety for the family he would leave behind). The alternative proposed by Fletcher would amount to the dereliction of this trust, and possibly the destruction of the penitent as a moral being, with his abandonment of trust in either man or God. Nor has the innocent man any reasonable grounds for complaint, since the information would not have been divulged, had not the situation of absolute trust been believed to exist.

Some of Fletcher's best-known illustrations are drawn from the field of sexual ethics. He gives two examples of cases in which adultery is involved. In the first a woman is asked to obtain a secretarial job in a western European city. She is then to engineer an affair with her married employer, as a result of which he can be blackmailed to disclose information about a hostile power. The second concerns a German woman in a Russian prison camp at the end of the Second World War, desperate to be reunited with her husband and two children in Berlin. The rules of the camp are that only pregnant women are to be returned to Germany immediately, and so she asks a friendly guard to impregnate her. The interesting thing about these two cases is the way in which Fletcher presents the moral dilemma. In the first 'it is a question of patriotic prostitution and personal integrity. In this case, how was she to balance loyalty as an American citizen over against her ideal of sexual integrity?' In the latter, exclusive attention is given to the mother and her family, and how their anxieties for one another's safety disappear with the reunion. The guard is simply mentioned in passing as the instrument of impregnation, just as the married employer is simply noted as a source of information. Yet, if anyone is being wronged in these two situations, it is surely most clearly these two individuals. For presumably the married employer, if he is to be led on into having an affair, must be deceived into believing that it is in fact a *love* affair, which it clearly is not. In the case of the camp guard we are not even told whether he was married or not. Even if he were single and performed the act without any deception having to be used, it would still not follow automatically that she had respected him as a person. For she might well be exposing him to harsh punitive measures if found out and, so far as the sexual act itself is concerned, she would be encouraging him in a casual attitude to sex of which, according to the story, she disapproves. Perhaps Fletcher would reply that he would be doing it as an act of pure charity, but if so, are we to envisage him as having a duty to impregnate all anxious mothers in the camp?

The considerations offered in the previous paragraph are obviously of varying degrees of force. However, it was only secondarily my intention to argue for a particular moral conclusion. My primary aim was to draw attention to the total inadequacy of Fletcher's style of reasoning, and in particular to challenge his claim that such a pattern of reasoning has got anything to do with love. Where it fails, as I hope the previous paragraph made clear, is in its failure to realize that love is essentially a matter of concern for individuals and that there can be no claim to such concern where some are exploited as mere instruments towards the realization of a greater good, without any attention or respect being given to their *particular* needs and welfare. In other words, Fletcher may be able to claim that it is the most productive way of proceeding (in the sense of quantitatively producing the most good) or the most fair (in the sense of benefitting the most number of people). What he cannot claim is that love is the guiding principle. At the most mundane level, English usage is against him. We don't talk about 'loving humanity' but about loving individuals. Admittedly, we do sometimes speak of loving ideals or, say, the Church, but this is very much a secondary usage, and even in these cases the notion of exploitation is excluded. One doesn't, for instance, exploit art in order to create art, if one truly loves art. But perhaps the most fundamental reason why Fletcher's account is unacceptable — ignoring specifically Christian considerations which we shall come to later — is the fact that love is an emotion. It is wellnigh impossible to have an emotional commitment to humanity *en masse*, as distinct from the particular individuals whom one encounters.

One final word on Fletcher. Nowhere does his lack of respect for the individual emerge more clearly than in his chapter, 'Love and Justice are the same'. For he tells us that President Truman's decision to drop atomic bombs on Hiroshima and Nagasaki was based on 'a vast scale of agapeistic calculus', without even noting, in passing, the thousands of innocent lives that were lost thereby. Not only that, but Christ himself is criticized. Commenting on the story of the anointing at Bethany in which a woman anoints Jesus with a costly ointment (Mark 14:3—9; John 12:1—8), he remarks that 'if we take the story as it stands, Jesus was wrong and the disciples were right'. The point is that the ointment might have been sold and the money raised given to the poor, but, when the disciples bring this to Jesus' attention, he merely comments: 'Let her alone; why trouble ye her? she hath wrought a good work on me.' But, so far from either challenging the authority of Jesus or, as Fletcher later does, the authenticity of the remark, what the Bethany incident does is to throw into highlight the true nature of love as contrasted with Fletcher's analysis. For, even if the woman is not to be identified with the 'sinner' of St Luke's gospel (Luke 7:36–50), to whom Jesus said, 'Her sins, which are many, are forgiven; for she loved much,' the reason for Jesus' acceptance of both anointings is surely the same: since the women chose this way to express their love or contrition, the only response of love is to accept the intended meaning, irrespective of how little it contributes to the greatest good of the greatest number. To do otherwise to a human being in such a situation would be to reject the unique expression of her as an individual, to stamp upon what was perhaps the most significant point in her moral development as a person.

With Christian imitations of Marxism I shall make fundamentally the same criticism. Christian Marxists fail to see love as a commitment to treating each and every individual involved with respect rather than just a dispensable part in an overall calculus. But, before developing such criticisms, I must first acknowledge the positive features of its most popular contemporary version, Liberation theology. To begin with, it is encouraging to find such a wealth of theological reflection coming from parts of the world that have hitherto remained dormant. Gustavo Gutierrez' minor classic *A Theology of Liberation*, José Miranda's *Marx and the Bible*, Hugo Assmann's *Practical Theology of Liberation*, Juan Luis Segundo's *The Liberation of Theology*, as well as the Protestant José Bonino's *Revolutionary Theology Comes of Age* (perhaps the best general introduction to the whole movement), are all evidence of growing Third World theological maturity. In addition, there is the related phenomenon of Black theology. One thinks here particularly of the American James Cone, author of *God of the Oppressed*, and the South African, Allan Boesak, author of *Black Theology, Black Power*. The fact that this represents only a small selection of the books published under these banners in the past ten years leaves one in no doubt about the extent of Marxist influence on current thinking among under-privileged Christians, a fact that is highly significant when one recalls that, whereas in 1900 85 per cent of Christians lived in Europe and North America, by the year AD 2000, according to current estimates, this will have been reduced to 42 per cent, with the majority coming from the Third World.

But it is not just the sheer bulk of writing which is impressive. There is undoubtedly a passionate concern to secure justice for the poor and oppressed. This is a healthy corrective to the automatic endorsement of the *status quo*, so long the norm for Latin American Catholicism despite the appalling conditions of deprivation so frequently found there. No such acknowledgement is made in Edward Norman's critique in his 1978 Reith Lectures, *Christianity and the World Order*. Indeed Norman denies any political implications to Christianity, declaring that 'the very thing religion ought to provide is lacking in our day' — 'a sense of the ultimate worthlessness of human expectation of a better life on earth'. The call for human rights, in his view, amounts to no more than aping of secular humanism. But this just won't do. The primary place accorded by Liberation theologians to the Exodus, with its liberation of the Hebrews from oppressive slavery in Egypt, is no accident. For there Yahweh is depicted as taking decisive action to rectify social injustice: 'And the Lord said, I have surely seen the affliction of my people which are in Egypt, and have heard their cry by reason of their taskmasters; for I know their sorrows; and I am come down to deliver them out of the hand of the Egyptians' (Exodus 3:7—8). Equally pertinent are the numerous prophetic denunciations of injustice, of which Miranda especially makes much (e.g.

11

Isa. 5:1—9; Jer. 22:13—19; Hos. 10:12—13; Amos 4:1—3; Mic. 3:8—12).

It is a commonplace to set against such passages what is alleged to be the purely personal morality of Jesus, as also the submissiveness to authority that seems to be enjoined by Paul in such passages as Romans 13 — 'Let every soul be subject unto the higher powers. For there is no power but of God; the powers that be are ordained of God' (v.1). Liberation theologians exhibit much ingenuity in trying to make the New Testament endorse the more activist political policies suggested by the Old. Two main types of argument may be distinguished: the reinterpretation of Christ's teaching and an argument based on the Marxist analysis of action or 'praxis'.

Gutierrez, for example, adopts the version in Luke, 'Blessed are the poor', rather than that in Matthew, 'Blessed are the poor in spirit', and comments that, since the Beatitudes are delivered in the context of the arrival of the Kingdom of God, this in effect must be a proclamation that 'the elimination of the exploitation and poverty that prevent the poor from being fully human has begun'. Again, Miranda comments on the famous 'camel and eye of the needle' passage (Luke 18:25) as follows: 'It is impossible to interpret this statement as directed against the distribution of differentiating ownership which DE FACTO prevails and not against DE IURE differentiating ownership as such'. As a final example one might mention Sobrino's remark in his book, *Christology at the Crossroads*: 'Strikingly enough, Jesus' harshest condemnations are not directed against the individual sinner . . . they are directed against the collective sins that create a situation contrary to the kingdom . . . There is poverty because the rich do not share their wealth. There is religious oppression because the priests impose intolerable burdens on people . . . There is political oppression because the rulers rule despotically'; and so he goes on to suggest that Jesus' primary concern must have been to change the social situation.

But such arguments fail to carry conviction. Apart from the historical improbability of such root and branch political change being contemplated at this time or social structures being seen to have such a key role, the available historical evidence points in a rather different direction. The fact that Jesus' followers continue to go to the Temple after his death makes it dubious whether he ever challenged the authority of the Temple *per se*, rather than particular abuses. Similarly, though Mark 10:42—5 might be read as an attack on traditional notions of authority, the New English Bible is surely right to read it as an attack on abuse of power — 'lord it over their subjects and . . . make them feel the weight of authority'. That Jesus accepts a traditional notion of secular authority is shown elsewhere by the fact that he gladly accepts the comparison made by the centurion between his own authority and that of Jesus (Matt. 8:9—10). Finally, so far as Luke 18:25 is concerned, its wider context indicates a contrast between trust in riches and a child-like faith (cf. Luke 18:17) rather than any revolutionary implications. Even if exploitation through riches was being referred to, it would not follow that wealth in itself has this destructive power in our very different social conditions. In short, then, Miranda's claim that there is 'an underlying profound affinity' with Marxism is utter nonsense. Certainly Jesus did not hesitate to attack abuse of power. But, equally, there is no specific programme for social reform.

Liberation theology's second main type of argument is likewise flawed by carrying a perfectly legitimate point to extremes. It is based on the Marxist conception of institutionalized or structural violence, the notion that simply in virtue of being part of a particular social structure one is acting violently in the sense of harming others, just as much as if one had taken up arms against them. Cone, for example, comments: 'It is important to point out that no one can be non-violent in an unjust society. . . Concretely, ours is a situation in which the only option we have is that of deciding whose violence we will support — that of the oppressors or the oppressed.' Segundo carries the argument a stage further by arguing that Jesus in his own life must therefore have performed violent acts, since it is inherent

13

in the nature of love to exclude some from consideration in order to devote more attention to others.

> We are able to love our neighbours to the extent that we keep other human beings from showing up as neighbours on our horizon. To strip the latter of being neighbours, we resort to the familiar mechanism of treating them as FUNCTIONS rather than as persons . . . Now no one can doubt that this mechanism DOES VIOLENCE to the one and indivisible reality of those persons. (*The Liberation of Theology*, p. 160)

There is undoubtedly a measure of truth in this notion of institutionalized violence. We are responsible for harm to others, more dreadful than many forms of physical violence, simply in virtue of the station we hold in life and the causal link between that station and the harm being done. This remains true whether we are aware of the causal link or not, though obviously in the latter case our culpability is lessened. Examples are too numerous to mention, though they are seldom entirely straightforward. A complex instance would be the extent of our corporate responsibility for the situation in the Third World. Gratitude is certainly due to Liberation theology for insisting that the concept be given a prominent position in any Christian ethical analysis. But Segundo reduces the whole notion to a farce. In no sense can it be claimed that Jesus acted violently simply in virtue of loving some and not others. For there is a basic difference between excluding some from attention even though one is responsible for their situation, and doing so simply because one has not enough personal resources or energy to deal with their needs as well. In short, while one must admit the existence of institutionalized violence, it is not so ubiquitous as to demand assent to the proposition that all ethics must necessarily be political.

However, even if neither of these two arguments had been of any force, there would still have been good grounds for insisting, as against Norman's point of view, that Christian ethics must have some social dimension in a concern for justice. First, Christ's teaching has always to be set in the context of the Old Testament, which is assumed throughout. Indeed, much of it would be inexplicable otherwise, e.g. the meaning of the term, 'Son of Man'. This applies equally to his ethical teaching and, as we have seen, there is no doubt about the Old Testament's emphasis on justice. Secondly, the very fact that Jesus' teaching concentrates on love shows that there is an underlying concern for justice present. For justice is surely simply the negative side of love's positive aspect. That is to say, justice is a matter of eliminating harm that is being done to others, whereas love is concerned with the realization of some positive good that is not simply the entitlement of the person benefited. Thus one cannot claim to love and at the same time ignore a person's just claims upon oneself. That being so, the explanation of why Christ so seldom refers explicitly to the demands of justice is not hard to find. They are assumed, and the challenge of his teaching is to invite us to go a stage beyond them.

It remains now to note the principal deficiency of Liberation theology. At this point one is tempted to follow the Spaniard, Alfredo Fierro, in his critique, *The Militant Gospel*, and label this the degeneration into 'rhetorical theology', since so much of it savours of preaching rather than rigorous analysis and argument. But there is a much more serious flaw, one it shares with situation ethics. That is the way in which it is enticed by its secular original along the path of regarding particular individuals as dispensable, whether or not they have done anything to deserve forfeiture of their rights, and even if one has entered into certain types of commitments to them. The cause seems to be an illegitimate extension of the notion of institutional violence in that it conveniently enables one to pronounce everyone guilty in advance of anything they do. Cone, for example, remarks:

White oppressors [by which he means all whites] must be excluded from this black ethical dialogue,

15

because they cannot be trusted. . . . Few if any whites can accept this. They will say that it is neither fair nor Christian. But we do not need to debate the meaning of fairness or Christianity with our oppressors. For they, of all people, have not earned the right to utter these words. (*God of the Oppressed*, pp. 216–17)

Indeed, in his earlier book, *A Black Theology of Liberation*, he had even gone so far as to say that 'if Christ is present today actively risking all for the freedom of man, he must be acting through the most radical elements of Black Power'. It is a short step from this to regard some particular Caucasian as merely an inconvenient obstacle on the way to this freedom. Even a more representative figure like Gutierrez is not far behind, with his suggestion that commitment to the class struggle must take precedence over any feeling of identification with one's fellow members in the Church.

REFORMATION INADEQUACIES: LUTHER AND CALVIN

Having seen the unsatisfactoriness of imitating secular ethics, we turn now to an examination of the resources of Christianity's past ethical tradition. The Reformation, being such a decisive point of divergence, would seem the obvious point to begin, though it should be noted that in this matter at least, as I shall demonstrate in the next chapter, Anglicanism remains unreformed. Given the doctrinal diversity that now exists within all the denominations, however, there would seem to be no reason why Lutherans or Calvinists today should feel obliged necessarily to defend the ethical positions of Luther and Calvin as outlined below. Indeed, to a considerable extent this has already happened. Paul Tillich was the most influential Lutheran theologian this century, but he would hardly have endorsed the view of the image of God in man which I ascribe to Luther. Again, Paul Ramsey is a Methodist, but much of the inspiration for his ethical writings comes from traditional Catholic analysis. As a final example of this modern freedom, one may observe that in practice Joseph Fletcher belongs to the Anglo-Catholic tradition, though this is certainly not reflected in his moral position.

The contrast between traditional Lutheran and Catholic ethics can be seen most effectively by quoting two Latin maxims from that time. Luther in one of his letters writes to Melanchthon: *'Esto peccator et pecca fortiter'* — 'Be a sinner and sin bravely'. The Holy Roman Emperor, Ferdinand I, who is known to have been a pious Roman Catholic, adopted as his motto the ancient adage: *'Fiat iustitia et ruat caelum'* — 'Let justice be done, though the heavens fall.' The precise nature of the contrast will emerge in due course, but first we must clarify what Luther meant.

When set in its proper context Luther's meaning seems less startling than appears at first sight. He was advising Melanchthon:

> If you are a preacher of grace, then preach a true and not a fictitious grace; if grace is true, you must bear a true and not a fictitious sin. God does not save people who are only fictitious sinners. Be a sinner and sin boldly, but believe and rejoice in Christ even more boldly, for he is victorious over sin, death and the world. As long as we live in this world we have to sin. . . . It is enough that by the riches of God's glory we have come to know the Lamb that takes away the sin of the world. (Letter 91: August 1, 1521)

In other words, Luther is not urging us to sin, but pointing out that in this world at least we have no choice but to do so, fallen creatures that we are. The moral law thus appears in what he regards as its proper or pedagogical (teaching) use, as a means of convicting us of our sin, of our total inability to live up to the standard demanded of us, and so of our need for total reliance on God's forgiveness, rather than any attempt to justify ourselves in his eyes by what we achieve through our own action. But, if this much can be said in defence of Luther, the overall effect of his teaching was nonetheless seen even by contemporaries,

17

such as Erasmus, as an incitement to sin, in the sense of legitimizing the acceptance of less than perfect, and so sinful, solutions to moral dilemmas. Even today his influence in this direction is displayed most powerfully in the writings of the most distinguished contemporary Lutheran ethicist, Helmut Thielicke.

It is interesting to consider why this is so. There would seem to be two main reasons. First, perhaps the most basic contrast of all in Luther's theology is that between Law and Gospel and, however profound a result this produces theologically in his exposition of the doctrine of justification by faith, ethically the whole contrast is a complete disaster. For it leads Luther to see the moral law, specific guides to conduct, in essentially negative terms. Either its role is pedagogical, as we have seen, or at most it has a political or coercive function in acting as a restraint on sin — what Luther calls 'God's rule with his left hand', as distinct from his 'proper work with his right', in revealing the need for grace. This realm of creation is then contrasted with the realm of redemption where love alone holds sway. But, since the Christian is a member of both and God is author of both, the Christian is obliged to circumscribe his acts of love by the demands of the created order. The result is that love is confined to a very small area of personal morality, and the basic guide to action becomes the second use of the law, its political use in preventing worse from happening. Little wonder then that Lutheran expectations for conduct are low.

But there is a second, deeper reason which explains Luther's pessimism about ethics. It is his belief about the extent of the Fall. For, perhaps in order to preclude any possibility of justification by works, he denies that any trace of natural goodness remains in fallen man. Referring us to Ephesians (4:21—4), he comments that man is in the image of the devil until he is redeemed by Christ. With such a view of the created order it is hardly surprising that a major role is assigned to constraint or that he believes that the most that can reasonably be expected is the realization of the lesser of two evils.

18

Thielicke, in his major three volumed work, *Theological Ethics*, admits the need for some correction to Luther, particularly in the light of the German Church's ready acceptance of Hitler's rise to power. He does so by what he calls 'the eschatological corrective', according to which, instead of envisaging a limited area where love can act without hindrance, he sees the realm of redemption calling into question the entire realm of creation, not in the sense of necessarily demanding very different conduct, but as always putting a question mark against it to indicate its provisional character, including the provisional character of attempts to act out the demands of love in this world. The result is a more radical Lutheranism, but one which is, if anything, even more committed than Luther to the inevitability of flawed, sinful solutions since even love, if it is to be lived out in this world, 'is obviously going to be all tied up with "hacking" and "strangling", with "judging", "punishing" and "repaying",' i.e. with provisional solutions. Thielicke's favourite word for this is in fact 'compromise', and he sees such compromises as the only viable option in the light of what our fallen nature is like: 'It has the significance of a "necessity", which includes the fact that what I am necessarily will out.'

Two examples of what this means in practice will suffice. He interprets Christ's teaching on marriage (Mark 10:2–12) not as abrogating the Mosaic permission for divorce, but rather as endorsing it as a divine concession to the 'hardness' of men's hearts. 'In this world . . . the radical command of creation ['from the beginning of creation God made them male and female . . . And they twain shall be one flesh'] could only issue in terror and chaos. The world is so alienated from the divine plan that it would be shattered and destroyed by it, did not God cause the grace of his accommodating intervention to triumph over the original claim' (*Foundations*, p. 571). On the question of nuclear weapons, Thielicke's discussion is complex, but basically he sees the issue as a choice between evils: 'It is simply a question of choosing between two evils . . . We must judge which alternative poses the greater danger: having an atomic power on one side and a vacuum on the other, or having a balance of atomic potential which . . . will always be precarious and uncertain so long as it is controlled by fallible men' (*Politics* p. 487). Nowhere does he consider the moral implications of the tremendous loss of innocent life which would ensue in the event of nuclear war, and indeed he argues strongly against unilateralism on the grounds that it would represent a fundamental infringement of the second use of the law: 'It is a decision against the Noachic order of the world [a reference to Genesis 9:5] in which arbitrary and unlimited power is to be restrained by further power.'

Constrast all this now with the Catholic position, as epitomized in Ferdinand's maxim: 'Let justice be done, though the heavens fall.' Indeed, Catholic ethics is often caricatured as amounting to no more than a series of absolute prohibitions, 'whatever the consequences' – a caricature that receives some support when one thinks of the standard Catholic position on the two issues which we used to illustrate Thielicke's views. Divorce is ruled out and only annulments are contemplated (a declaration that there was no proper marriage there in the first place). Likewise, there is an absolute prohibition on the intentional killing of the innocent, and so the nuclear bombing of cities is forbidden. That equating Catholic ethics with rules is nonetheless a caricature is something which we shall attempt to demonstrate shortly. But, first, attention must be drawn to the underlying source of the dispute between Lutheran and Catholic ethics.

It is a matter of one's view of God. Luther's view was that the image of God in man has been obliterated and that, even when justified by faith, so inherently sinful is his situation, there will be no choice available but that of tainted compromise. To this, the Catholic responds by asking two questions. First, would a good God really allow all trace of his image to disappear from natural man? Secondly, even if this were so, would a good God really allow man to be placed in situations where the only choice is between evil and evil?

Both questions raise a large number of theological issues, which we have not the space to deal with here. On the first, the Catholic tradition has consistently denied that the Fall was total. Unfortunately, it has sometimes expressed this in terms of a contrast between nature and grace and given the impression that the divine aid that constitutes grace amounts to no more than, as it were, the icing on the wedding cake. But this distortion has been corrected in contemporary Catholic theology in, for instance, Karl Rahner's contention that all goodness stems from grace and that 'nature' is a purely abstract concept (the building blocks, as it were, that need the co-operation of man and God before anything good can come of them). With this correction, there is all the more reason for seeing the image as being far from obliterated. For all men will then be seen as experiencing to some degree the directing hand of God towards goodness, whether they are aware of it or not. As such, it is surely more realistic than the Lutheran account. Goodness does undoubtedly exist in non-Christians — sometimes to a very high degree. It is also more loyal to the Scriptures (cf. Romans 2:13—15). Finally, it safeguards the goodness of God. He has not allowed his creation to become essentially depraved or corrupt.

So far as our other question is concerned, there are certainly biblical passages which appear to suggest that the whole of creation, not just man, participated in the Fall (e.g. Rom. 8:19—22). But this is a very different matter from conceding that a perfectly good God would allow the situation to get so out of control that man is faced with no option but to do evil, especially if this were to be seen as the norm. Catholic moral theology has always rejected this possibility. The result has been carefully elaborated distinctions between intended and unintended consequences of action, particularly as exemplified in the so-called 'doctrine of double effect'. This is a distinction to which we shall have to return later. In the meantime, let the reader simply reflect on the travesty of a moral management of the world which is implied, if the Lutheran position is accepted.

It remains now to say something about that other great Reformation figure, Calvin. It is commonly supposed that he is at a further remove from Catholicism than Luther, especially given his well-known doctrine of the total depravity of man. Ironically he is in fact much nearer in terms of ethics. To begin with, it should be noted that it does not follow from his view of total depravity that the divine image has been totally obliterated. Far from it. What remains is a relic or remnant in the shape of God's gifts to man (the building blocks), but which, however, man inevitably misuses (hence total depravity). Indeed, so confident is Calvin of the survival of the image in sinful man that he does not hesitate to use it to underpin our obligation to treat all persons as sacred. As part of a rather moving section of the *Institutes* he remarks: 'The Lord commands us to do good to all without exception, though the greater part, if estimated by their own merit, are unworthy of it. But scripture gives us an excellent reason when it tells us that we are not to look to what men themselves deserve but to attend to the image of God which is present in all men and to which we owe all honour and love.' It is a sentiment with which Catholic ethicists would find themselves in complete agreement, even if they would not also be willing to endorse his view that the potential present in the image is entirely perverted in unredeemed man.

But, not only is Calvin nearer to the Catholic position on the question of the divine image, he also exhibits a far more positive attitude to specific ethical injunctions. For he accepts what Melanchthon first labelled 'the third use of the law', and indeed regards it as its principal use. This didactic use is exhibited in its ability to instruct the Christian in how to lead the good life, and indeed one way of making the contrast between Luther and Calvin most explicit would be to say that, whereas for Luther ethics was all a matter of justification, of convicting us of our need for God's forgiveness through faith, with Calvin it is essentially a matter of our sanctification, the perfecting of the image through the indwelling Spirit. That

22

explains why Calvin devotes so much attention in the *Institutes* to the exposition of the Decalogue, the Ten Commandments. Of course, his attempt to apply the moral law in detail in the city of Geneva cannot exactly be described as a success. But this should not blind us to the fact that, unlike Luther, he not only saw positive value in ethical rules, but also correctly located that value in religious rather than merely secular terms. For, if the divine image means anything, it must surely at least mean the potentiality to conform ourselves to the moral will of God. At all events, it has always been integral to the Catholic view that it is by such growing conformity that we are prepared for heaven.

Yet, one must add a note of qualification. For, despite Calvin's acknowledgement of the positive role of the ethical life, it is an insight that is pursued to no great depth. Moral rules exist simply as divine commands, and no more, he feels, needs to be said. Admittedly, Catholic ethics has sometimes been presented in exactly the same kind of way, particularly at the popular level. But the Catholic tradition is much richer than this. It has always insisted that the Christian moral life is being lived at its fullest when its demands are no longer seen as externally imposed commands but as the natural spontaneous expression of the person's interior life. There is a passing allusion to this when Calvin refers to Christians having 'the law written and engraved on their hearts by the finger of God', but it is not something he makes anything of. This is a pity because, as we shall see in the next chapter, it is an important plank in any adequate defence of Christian ethics. For the moment, simply note the essential arbitrariness of commands which fail to find a basis in the natural potentialities of the individual and which he is consequently unable to interiorize as his very own.

FURTHER READING

On Utilitarianism and Marxism

John Stuart Mill, *Utilitarianism* (ed. Mary Warnock), Fontana/Collins, 1962 (includes selections from Bentham and Mill)

L. Trotsky, J. Dewey and G. Novack, *Their Morals and Ours*, Path-finder Press, New York, 1973

On situation ethics and liberation theology

Joseph Fletcher, *Situation Ethics,* SCM, 1966

José Bonino, *Doing Theology in a Revolutionary Age*, Fortress Press, 1975 (English edition: *Revolutionary Theology Comes of Age,* SPCK, 1975)

James Cone, *God of the Oppressed*, Seabury Press, NY, 1975; SPCK, 1977

On Luther and Calvin

Helmut Thielicke, *Theological Ethics*, 3 vols, Eerdmans, Grand Rapids, Michigan, 1979 esp. Vol. 1 *Foundations* and Vol. 2 *Politics*

John Calvin, *Institutes of the Christian Religion* book 2, chapters 7 and 8; available in the *Library of Christian Classics*, vol. XX, Westminster Press, Philadelphia, 1960

2 The Catholic and Anglican Answer

The previous chapter dealt with what may well have seemed an essentially negative task, the location of inadequacies in alternative positions to that now to be presented. But in the process, not merely has the reader been made forcibly aware of the great variety of viewpoints within Christian ethics, he has also been alerted to certain positive features which any satisfactory account of Christian ethics will require. These can perhaps be conveniently reduced to two basic demands. First, while a concern for both love and justice are integral to the Christian vision, these must be treated in a way that is compatible with respect for each and every individual having a unique worth in their own right — not just as a means to some further end, a mere item in a larger calculation. Secondly, Christian ethics must be built on the assumption that God's creation is fundamentally good, and so it will reflect something of the way in which God has made man, not the inherent sinfulness of the world (Luther) nor the imposition of external commands (Calvin). These two requirements are fully met in the four main principles of Catholic morality.

But, first, a word of explanation must be given with regard to the title of this chapter. This book forms part of a series to celebrate the one hundred and fiftieth anniversary of the beginnings of the Oxford Movement in 1833, a date often regarded as the decisive landmark in the history of Catholic Anglicanism. However, the chapter is not called 'the Catholic Anglican answer', but 'the Catholic and Anglican answer'. This is deliberate, because, at least so far as Christian ethics is concerned, one can plausibly maintain that, in so far as Anglicanism has had any moral theology of its own, all its leading figures have adopted a Catholic approach, irrespective of whether they were Catholic or not in their general doctrinal position. Nor is the explanation for this hard to find. It is due to the ubiquitous influence of St Thomas Aquinas (1224—74), undoubtedly the greatest moral theologian the Church has ever produced. Thus, at the end of the sixteenth century we find Richard Hooker, the classical exponent of an Anglican middle way, deeply influenced by him in his theory of law. A century later there occurs the first serious attempt at Anglican moral theology under the two Charles in the phenomenon known as Caroline moral theology. Some of its most distinguished representatives were Puritans (e.g. Richard Baxter) but, despite this, Aquinas' influence is everywhere to be seen. This is especially true of the two most famous, Robert Sanderson and Jeremy Taylor, though the latter expresses himself more critically. It is important, however, to note the real object of Caroline criticism. The most thorough recent examination of their position, H. R. McAdoo's *The Structure of Caroline Moral Theology*, distinguishes a traditionalist and a reforming strain, and this may convey the impression that there was a more radical cleavage from the past than in fact was the case. For it was not just their emphasis on natural law and conscience which exhibited continuity with Aquinas, but also what McAdoo calls 'the reforming strain', their critique of the distinction between venial and mortal sin and emphasis on the pursuit of holiness. This is because the real object of their attack here (as another book on the subject, Thomas Woods' *English Casuitical Divinity*, is at pains to point out) was contemporary Jesuits, not Aquinas. Indeed, their attack on sacramental confession can rightly be seen as having a medieval basis, in Thomas' emphasis on the indispensable role of morality in bringing us to the vision of God. What they objected to was not the practice in itself, but the lack of seriousness which accompanied contemporary Roman practice, especially its failure to bring about the pursuit of holiness, an objective with which Aquinas would have been in complete agreement.

The eighteenth century then witnessed the Church of England's most lasting contribution to ethics, Joseph Butler's *Fifteen Sermons*, first published in 1726. Butler has been described as 'Aristotle, clad in a diaphanous mantle of Christianity'. This is very unfair, as Butler's Christianity has both enriched and considerably altered the original Aristotelian position, but it does draw attention to the continuity with Aquinas. For Aquinas too used the philosophy of Aristotle as a framework in which to present the true nature of Christian ethics. That the influence of Aristotle and Butler provided the Oxford Movement with continuity of approach, there can be no doubt. For, unlike the Caroline divines, there was very little, if any, direct acquaintance with Aquinas. But Newman described Butler as 'the greatest name in the Anglican Church' and Aristotle as 'the great Master', and the influence of both shines through in his ethical reflections. Again, Keble absorbed the ideas of Aquinas indirectly through his editing of Hooker's *Ecclesiastical Polity* and his knowledge of the Caroline divines. Some may doubt whether the Oxford Movement had any moral theology at all. Certainly, it was not their primary interest. But such doubts are soon dispelled by even a cursory reading of the Tractarians' writings, especially when it is remembered that certain elements were present in their thought only seminally that were to have a profound effect on subsequent moral and political discussion within the Church.

Just to complete the story so far as the Anglican Church is concerned, it remains to mention the names of F. D. Maurice (1805–72), Charles Gore (1853–1932) and Kenneth Kirk (1886–1954). In Kirk's case, the Aristotelian influence is dominant, but with the other two it is the other major Greek philosopher who holds sway. But, though the differences between Plato and Aristotle are great, it is a shared feature that produced most influence on these two men, the demand that all morality must be based on an analysis of human nature. It should also be noted that Maurice's ethics are essentially Catholic in approach, despite his own ambivalent attitude to the Oxford Movement generally.

Sufficient indication has now been given of the way in which my claim that Anglican moral theology has always been essentially Catholic could be defended in detail. It assumes that Catholic moral theology has always been Thomist in approach. That this has been incontestably true in the Roman communion at least since the sixteenth century with the great Thomist commentators, Cajetan and Vitoria, would seem beyond doubt. And it remains true today despite the very different manner of expression used by Rome's most influential contemporary moral theologian, Bernard Häring. It is also interesting to note that in the brief synopsis of the history of the subject which opens his latest major work (*Moral Theology for Priests and Laity*), Newman is given a key role, thus confirming that our view of the contribution of the Oxford Movement is not simply idiosyncratic: 'No moral theologian can ignore the great vision of Newman on conscience and on genuine religious authority.'

But enough has now been said on the history of the subject. We turn to an examination of the four main planks on which, in our view, the Catholic position is based.

NATURAL LAW AND CONSCIENCE

Readers unfamiliar with the history of Christian ethics may find it rather shocking that two pagan philosophers have had such a profound influence, even if this influence has been largely mediated through St Thomas Aquinas. Paul Ramsey, in his book *Basic Christian Ethics*, attacks the whole notion of natural law on the grounds that it would fail to provide a 'distinctively Christian' ethics, and one suspects that the hostility of so many Protestants stems from a mistaken belief that natural law makes the Scriptures and particularly the teaching of Jesus himself redundant. But such objections can last only for so long as one fails to take account of the way in which ethical reflection proceeds.

The German philosopher, Immanuel Kant (1724—1804), once remarked that 'even the Holy One of the Gospel must first be compared with our idea of moral perfection before we can recognise him as such'. Now there is a measure of truth in this, but it is at best a dangerous half-truth. The element of truth is that, unless we had first formed some conception of moral goodness and of our own failure to live up to that ideal, there would be nothing about the life of Christ that could evoke an answering chord in ourselves. God's message to man would be a totally alien product that he could only impose upon us, not expect us to respond to freely, however inadequately. It comes therefore as of little surprise that the leading Reformation figures place such emphasis on predestination, to the detriment of free will. God can only arbitrarily create a response; for in the Reformation view there is nothing in man that could begin to reach up to God. But such a position makes a complete mockery of the divine government of the world. For it robs God of any justice in his dealings with men. Men must have freedom to respond or not to God's grace, and this means that man must be able to perceive something of God's moral purposes for his creation, prior to any explicit awareness of his saving will for mankind. That is why Catholic moral theology has always wisely insisted on the existence of natural law, the availability of moral truth prior to revelation.

Before we go on to explain what is meant by 'natural law' in rather more detail, the error in Kant's claim must be made clear. Newman strongly endorses the position I have just outlined. He speaks of this life as one in which 'man is in a state of trial . . . for which he is to give an account hereafter', and he deduces from this that man must have a free ability to exercise his will since 'without private judgment there is no responsibility'. He then goes on to make the following highly pertinent comment:

Our parents and teachers are our first informants concerning the next world; and they elicit and cherish the innate sense of right and wrong which acts as a guide co-ordinately with them. By degrees they resign their place to the religious communion, or Church, in which we find ourselves, while the inward habits of truth and holiness which the moral sense has begun to form, react upon that inward monitor, enlarge its range, and make its dictates articulate, decisive and various. (*Via Media*, 1, 5, 3.)

The point Newman is making is that, although in order to allow human responsibility one must grant the existence of a moral sense independent of relevation, it by no means follows from this that revelation, has no role to play. Far from it. For, as the passage makes clear, the development of one's conscience is not an automatic thing. It needs first to be 'elicited' and 'cherished' by our parents, but can then be 'enlarged' still further in its 'range', if the individual chooses to put himself in the context of the community of the Church where the vision of Christ, as presented in the Church's Scriptures, can not merely correct his perceptions but challenge him to lift them to an altogether higher plane.

Newman draws attention to the tremendous joy that can exist for a Christian as he sees the continuity of God's purposes, as his moral vision is enlarged and confirmed by the teaching of Christ.

There is, perhaps, no greater satisfaction to the Christian than that which arises from his perceiving that the Revealed system is rooted deep in the natural course of things, of which it is merely the result and completion; that his Saviour has interpreted for him the faint or broken accents of Nature; and that in them, so interpreted, he has, as if in some old prophecy, at once the evidence and the lasting memorial of the truths of the Gospel. (*University Sermons*, No, 2, p. 31)

But, the reader may be asking, can we continue to place such reliance on natural law and conscience? Such doubts are frequent today, even in Catholic circles, but they are quite unfounded, and indeed derive from a completely debased understanding of what is involved in the two concepts. So far as conscience is concerned, the Thomist tradition has never regarded it as the infallible voice of God within man. In fact, St Thomas distinguishes between what he calls 'synderesis' and 'conscientia'. The latter does deal with specific moral judgements, but it can, he admits, often go astray through either a failure of rationality, a failure to think clearly, or a failure of adequate nurture that produces blindness in one's choice of the principle on which one acts. Synderesis, by contrast, is concerned with the perception of highly general first principles and what follows from them, and it is only these highly general first principles that are regarded as self-evident, the most basic being that 'good should be done and evil avoided'. It is into this context that natural law fits. For, contrary to two common misconceptions, it has nothing to do either with law in the sense of highly specific injunctions to action, or with nature in the wider sense, e.g. arguing from the conduct of animals to the appropriate conduct for men. Rather, it is based on the view that human nature has been so fashioned by God that it is only by leading a moral life that certain basic demands of this nature can be satisfactorily realized. Natural law is thus the attempt to read off from those basic demands of human nature what the moral imperatives set by God in creating man might be.

No one nowadays would pretend that this is an easy task, but there seems no doubt that some such implications exist. For example, without some agreement about justice, human society would be impossible. This alone is enough to undermine the claim that since Darwin the idea of conscience must be rejected. For, since social existence is impossible without some notion of justice, there will inevitably be at least one principle of natural law reflected in any conceivable society's moral thinking, whether they choose to call it conscience or not. But, of course, much more is normally meant than this bare minimum — a bare minimum that is, incidentally, accepted by agnostic philosophers such as Sir Peter Strawson and Herbert Hart.

Let us return once more to Newman. Talking of a conscience operating in a heathen country, he remarks: 'It will of course realise in its degree those peculiar rewards of virtue which appetite cannot comprehend; and will detect in this world's events . . . a general connexion existing between right moral conduct and happiness, in corroboration of those convictions which the experience of its own private history has created' (Sermon, No. 2). In other words, the naturalist would claim that God has so structured our natures with various psychological needs that discontent is inevitable unless we pursue the moral path. It is an assumption which Plato and Aristotle shared, and that is why there is nothing inappropriate in their use by Christians. One needs, of course, to caution that happiness refers to one's life as a whole, not to particular isolated units of pleasure. There is no satisfactory modern equivalent to the Greek term *eudaimonia*, but perhaps the idea of an integrated, well-balanced person best conveys the sense or, alternatively, the self-actualized individual of American personalist psychologists such as Maslow. It is the search for an adequate modern translation which explains the relative absence of natural-law terminology from the pages of Häring, and the predominance of words such as 'wholeness' and 'integration'.

The plausibility of such an approach to ethics continues to be discussed by philosophers, and indeed naturalism has experienced something of a revival in recent years in secular philosophy. Its advantage for Christian ethics is that it makes continuing dialogue possible rather than reducing the Church to mere preaching. Inevitably there will be points at which the Christian will find himself forced to rely on theological assumptions, but it is important that this should be done consciously, and not just as a form of retreat. That at any rate will be my objective in subsequent chapters. It is also an aim with which Bishop Butler for the most part concurred in his impressive two sermons, 'Upon Human Nature', based on the text Romans 2:14.

Yet, in the last few lines one finds him retreating: 'Conscience and self-love, if we understand our true happiness, always lead us the same way. Duty and interest are perfectly coincident', he affirms, but then goes on, 'for the most part in this world, but entirely and in every instance if we take in the future, and the whole; this being implied in the notion of a good and perfect administration of things.' But even if we take the extreme instance of someone called to sacrifice his life for what he believes to be right, it still makes sense to claim that his life was happier as a result of the possession of those moral principles than it would otherwise have been. For he can look back on his life as fulfilled, with his present sacrifice as the completion and culmination of its meaning. By contrast, if the naturalist is right, the immoralist's life will be essentially one of frustrations and tensions caused by the unfulfilled, unintegrated aspects of his personality.

But, it may be objected, did not Christ say, 'if thy hand offend thee, cut it off' (Mark 9:43)? It is an objection Austin Farrer briefly raises in *Saving Belief*. As an illustration of the problem, one might mention the case of a daughter who devotes her life to looking after elderly, infirm parents, thereby stunting some possibilities of personal development. However, I do not think that this shows that the naturalist is wrong. What it does show is that the demands of certain dispositions that are central to such a personality — for example, love — may on occasion be such that a complete fulfilment of the personality is impossible.

Such a naturalist approach will, incidentally, solve one of the longest-standing dilemmas in Christian ethics, the so-called Euthyphro dilemma called after Plato's dialogue of that name in which he first presented the problem. It runs as follows: either God wills something because it is good, or something is good because God wills it. If the former is true morality will exist independently and antecedently of God; if the latter, morality becomes entirely abitrary, just a matter of the whims of God. Neither alternative sounds attractive, though both have

33

found favour among theologians. The solution is to say, with naturalism, that God has so ordained man's natural capacities that they can only obtain their proper fulfilment and deepest satisfaction by man leading a life that corresponds to what we would recognize as a moral life. For, if this is so, what is right and wrong can now be ascertained independently of direct reference to God's will, and so cannot be called arbitrary in that sense; nor can it be called arbitrary in the deeper sense of bearing no relation to the particular situation of the individual and his needs. Yet, at the same time an ultimate connection with the divine will is maintained, that is in no way arbitrary, the link between human nature and morality being based on God's loving concern for man. Even an atheist philosopher like John Mackie regards this as an adequate resolution of the traditional dilemma.

Perhaps Newman's greatest contribution to theology generally was the attention he drew to the development in doctrine after the closure of the canon of Scripture, something which we are even more aware of today, applying, as it does, to such major doctrines as Trinity and Incarnation. Newman did not contemplate its application to the moral sphere, but it is something we need to do. For we must contemplate not only the possibility of our consciences being enlarged by the Scriptures, but also the possibility of them being enlarged by the secular conscience. This cannot mean that the Church is free to challenge any of the central moral teachings of the Bible, but the notion can be seen to operate where the implications of those central teachings have not always been fully perceived. An obvious example is the status of women. The myth of Eve being created from a rib of Adam (Gen. 2:21–2) led Paul to draw certain implications about the status of women (e.g. 1 Cor. 11:7–9) that are incompatible with his fundamental declaration that 'there is neither male nor female; for ye are all one in Christ Jesus' (Gal. 3:28). Besides which, there are numerous situations on which the Bible makes no pronouncements, but upon which the Christian may be called to make ethical decisions. In these

34

cases he must rely on guidelines given by the basic biblical principles and interpret the empirical facts in the light of them. But the challenge of the secular conscience should certainly not be ignored. For it too is the creation of God just as much as his own.

FORMATION AND GROWTH IN HOLINESS

Of all the criticisms that are likely to be made of the previous section, perhaps the easiest to anticipate is that the Catholic has too optimistic a view of man and so fails to take sin seriously enough. Yet of all the accusations that could be launched against the Oxford Movement, none could be more unfair. Pusey's sermons reek of sin, and indeed he was only persuaded to give his course of sermons on 'Comforts to the Penitent', when the complaint went up that he was too negative in his approach. Again, the normally gentle Keble (in his *Letters of Spiritual Guidance*) attacks the Reformation doctrine of justification by faith for failing to take sin seriously enough, and does so in no uncertain terms: 'The tradition which goes by the name of Justification by faith and which in reality means that one who has sinned and is sorry for it, is as if he had not sinned, blights and benumbs one in every limb, in trying to make people aware of their real state.' Finally, Newman can probably claim the dubious distinction of enunciating the most severe pronouncement on the seriousness of sin ever made:

> The Church holds that it were better for sun and moon to drop from heaven, for the earth to fail, and for all the many millions who are upon it to die of starvation in extremest agony, so far as temporal affliction goes, than that one soul, I will not say, should be lost, but should commit one single venial sin, should tell one wilful untruth, though it harmed no one, or steal one poor farthing without excuse. (*Difficulties of Anglicans*, Lecture 8)

Newman is describing an inconceivable situation, and so

his comment must be judged more rhetorical flourish than fact. But behind the flourish there is a serious point, as the context of the passage makes abundantly clear. For Newman, as indeed for all the Tractarians, 'sin is the enemy of the soul', and so wrong action cannot be regarded lightly, because it will always reflect on the wider context of the warfare in which the Christian is engaged, whether his motives are being purified by the indwelling Spirit of God or proceeding from a corrupt heart. As Newman says in that same notorious passage: 'Good and evil . . . are not lights and shades passing over the surface of society, but living powers, springing from the depths of the heart.' He then refers us to Christ's words: 'That which cometh out of the man, that defileth the man. For from within, out of the heart of men, proceed evil thoughts . . .' etc. (Mark 7:20ff). He also quotes Jesus' comment that 'except your righteousness shall exceed the righteousness of the scribes and Pharisees, ye shall in no case enter into the kingdom of heaven' (Matt. 5:20) to show the intimate connection which exists between our ultimate salvation and the moral character which is being formed within us.

With this emphasis on the seriousness of external conduct as the expression of our real selves, there goes a conviction that the apparently trivial act can in fact have profound significance, because it may well make easier the creation of bad habits within us that adversely affect our ultimate destiny. In the third of his *University Sermons*, Newman asks: 'When the shortness of our probation is added to the serious thoughts already dwelt upon, who shall estimate the importance of every day and hour of a Christian's life in its bearing on his eternal destiny?' Likewise, Pusey warns (in a letter to Maria Trench) that the full significance of apparently insignificant conduct may only be seen in retrospect: 'The greater our Christian progress, the more we shall see our defects; things which in an early stage appear trifles assume a different character when our standard is raised, our mutual vision quickened and cleared by increased Christian experience and self-knowledge.'

All this on first hearing might sound suspiciously like an attempt to base our salvation on justification by works, that it is a matter of us exhibiting sufficient goodness such that God is then compelled to accept us. Fuel may well have been added to this suspicion by our earlier quotation of Keble's attack on the Reformation doctrine of justification by faith. But the object of the Tractarians' venom was not the Pauline doctrine (and it is certainly in St Paul), but the corruptions of it they saw in Reformation, and more particularly in contemporary Evangelical, presentations of the Reformation position. All that seems to have been demanded was the putting of one's trust in Christ, as though that were the end of the story of one's salvation. The result was that conversion was seen as an instantaneous act without further consequences, rather than the beginning of a transforming process that would last the rest of the individual's life. Insight into the continuing responsibility of the convert to respond to the work of the Spirit in him was therefore lost.

That is why Newman ends his sermon on 'Evangelical Sanctity the Completion of Natural Virtue' with both an emphasis on personal responsibility for our continuing response to God's work within us and a declaration that this must be set in the context of an ultimate dependence on faith in God's merciful love for men, as demonstrated by his reconciling act on the Cross.

> The day, we know, will come, when every Christian will be judged, not by what God has done for him, but by what he has done for himself: when, of all the varied blessings of Redemption, in which he was clad here, nothing will remain to him, but what he has incorporated in his own moral nature, and made part of himself. And, since we cannot know what measure of holiness will be then accepted in our own case, it is but left to us to cast ourselves individually on God's mercy in faith, and to look steadily, yet humbly, at the Atonement for sin which he has appointed. (*University Sermons*, No. 3, p. 53).

The indispensable role of God is thus by no means lost sight of in all this emphasis on responsibility and the need for growth in holiness. Indeed, it is just as clearly acknowledged by St Thomas Aquinas. For, the definition which he sees as 'comprising perfectly the whole notion of virtue' is as follows: 'Virtue is a good quality of mind by which one lives righteously, of which no one can make bad use, which God works in us without us.' The phrases, 'without us' leaves us in no doubt that the key actor involved is the Spirit within us transforming us. At the same time he goes on to add that 'without us' does not mean 'without our consent', and so his ideas are entirely congruent with the Tractarian emphasis on personal responsibility. The two sides of the coin are captured in the title given to this section, 'formation and growth in holiness'. It is formation, in that it is God who gives our characters shape; but it is also growth, in that he always acts with our consent and so change and improvement are inevitably gradual.

It is worth underlining yet again that this Catholic emphasis is also found in writers whose theology is otherwise not conspiciously Catholic. We have already mentioned the Caroline divines. John Wesley is another example. In his sermon on 'The Circumcision of the Heart', preached in the University Church, Oxford in 1733, he remarks: 'The circumcision of the heart is that habitual disposition of the soul, which in the sacred writings is termed 'holiness', which directly implies . . . being cleansed from sin . . . and by consequence the being endowed with those virtues which were also in Christ Jesus.' But, whether the insight comes from someone firmly entrenched within an overall Catholic position or not, the import remains the same, that with such a view of the Christian life there is a need for careful analysis of what constitutes right and wrong habits of mind. One cannot just rest content with the hints offered in the Bible; one must make explicit the implications of the biblical message.

This is what Aquinas attempts in the most impressive analysis of virtues and vices yet attempted, the 'Secunda Secundae' of his *Summa Theologiae*, that constitutes a

quarter of this extensive work. Traditionally, seven right habits of mind and seven wrong have been located. The seven virtues have been taken to be the four cardinal ones that play such a central role in Plato's *Republic*, justice, courage, prudence and temperance or self-restraint, plus the three theological virtues of 1 Corinthians 13, faith, hope and charity. The most corrosive vicious habits have been identified as the so-called 'seven deadly sins', easily remembered by the mnemonic, PLAGUES — P, pride; L, lust; A, avarice; G, gluttony; U (double U = W!), wrath or anger; E, envy; S, sloth. Whether these lists are entirely correct is a matter of secondary importance. A certain flexibility towards them is in any case evident within the Catholic tradition. For instance, the seven deadly sins began as eight, with dejection included in their number. Again, Newman speaks of 'faith, benevolence and justice, and temperance' as the 'ordinary virtues', whereas 'hope, charity and self-denial' are regarded as 'the peculiar fruits of the Spirit'.

The features that do seem important are the following. First, in contrast to contemporary secular morality, attention is overwhelmingly directed towards the inner man, to the intention which proceeds from the heart, rather than the outward act itself. The psychology of the individual thus becomes all important, what motivates him deep down, not just what appears on the surface. Secondly, in contrast to much popular Christian morality, including much popular Catholic morality, conformity to external rules is seen as but a poor substitute for conduct that is internally motivated, that comes from firmly entrenched habits, i.e. from one's virtuous dispositions. Now, of course, this is an ideal that very few Christians can expect to realize fully, and so rules must remain as a useful interim measure. But it should not be forgotten that in the Catholic view they are an interim measure, a mere temporary expedient, and that the saint will do spontaneously what most of us will perforce have to subsume under some rule. Given such a perspective, it becomes more readily explicable why Catholic ethics regards 'situation ethics' and related Protestant theories that make morals a matter of love alone as utterly shallow. On the grounds of Christian liberty, either they reduce ethics to one rule as with the agapeistic calculus of Fletcher or they suppose the immediate guidance of the Holy Spirit in each situation. But the true Christian freedom of which St Paul speaks, 'the glorious liberty of the children of God' (Rom. 8:21), will come not by abandoning rules, but by transcending them, as the mind of Christ is formed in us and they become part of our very selves.

Finally, attention must be drawn to the extent to which this emphasis on virtues and vices accords with naturalist assumptions. For, not only will morality, in this view, be very much the expression of the individual's real self; sin itself can be analysed as a perversion of man's true natural potentialities, and so the source of sin's power correctly located. This is why, as the Epistle to the Hebrews puts it, 'sin so easily besets us' (12:1). For it is by no means a totally unnatural grafting onto a quite different shoot. Rather, it is a turning aside from, and a misuse of, perfectly natural instincts which God has given us. Indeed, the instincts, of which the seven deadly sins are corruptions, are of such a fundamental kind that it is highly dubious whether mankind could survive without them. This is most obviously true of the sexual instinct and the appetite for food and drink, of which lust and gluttony are the perversions. But consider how important the acquisitive instinct is to the progress of society. Without it there would be no desire to acquire new information or new understandings. Avarice or greed is simply this natural God-given faculty misused. Or again, think how vital the pattern of work and rest is to our lives. Sloth is but the corruption of this divinely ordained rhythm. Another instance would be the way in which success in life is dependent on a healthy spirit of competitiveness; indeed, it is the most basic assumption of a capitalist society. Envy is its perversion. Similarly, determination or pugnacity, gritting your teeth and getting on with it, is indispensable when difficulties have to be faced. Unjustified anger, blowing your top over some minor obstacle, is its perversion. Nor is pride an exception. For it too is a corruption of something perfectly natural, the desire for esteem, the desire to be thought of some worth. Once again, its indispensability can scarcely be in doubt. Just think how sad the situation is of an individual lacking in all self-esteem, who can find no reason to value himself or his life. He is but a hollow shell, and some form of psychological disorder would seem the inevitable result. The Christian emphasis on humility does nothing to undermine this contention. It merely amounts to the demand that we acknowledge the source of our worth as deriving from the gracious activity of God working in us. The failure to see this has been the source of the mistake in humility's detractors, from the time of David Hume onwards.

Many other things could be said on this subject, as, for instance, that traditionally lust has been regarded as the least serious of the seven deadly sins, and pride as the most serious, the latter because it directs the attention inwards and away from recognition of one's dependence on God. But one thing cannot be omitted, and that is some reference to the renewed emphasis which the Oxford Movement placed on the role of the sacraments in the moral life. Probably no man did more to revive the practice of sacramental confession in the Church of England than Pusey, and indeed his last major work was an edition of Abbé Gaume's *Advice on Hearing Confessions*. The Eucharist too is given a major role in what he describes, in the introduction to his *Nine Sermons Preached Before the University of Oxford*, as one of the two 'central objects of those whom men call Tractarians', namely 'the promotion of holiness'. In his 1843 sermon on the Eucharist he declares that Christ 'can, if we be faithful and keep his gift which we receive, give such abundant strength to our rarer communions that they shall carry us through our forty days of trial, unto his own Holy Hill, and the vision of Himself in bliss'. Of course, both sacraments can be abused, and indeed with sacramental confession there is the same danger of which Keble spoke with reference to the Reformation doctrine of justification by faith — that it will

41

become merely automatic, a mere listing of sins rather than any serious attempt to deepen our spiritual perceptions, to enable us to see ourselves as we are seen. One thing is certain, that the most common failing of us all is self-deception, and, if that is so, all Christians must agree this much at least, that — whether we interpet James' injunction to 'confess your sins one to another' (5:16) as involving the presence of a priest or not — we do desperately need the help of others if the scales are to be removed from our eyes and moral progress be made.

LOVE AND THE SACREDNESS OF THE PERSON

In the previous chapter I was primarily concerned to attack the prevalent trend in contemporary ethics towards regarding the individual as a mere unit in some overall sum and so as dispensable — just a means to some further end. I showed it to be a claim made about the nature of love itself, as with situation ethics. It is an interpretation already anticipated by John Stuart Mill himself: 'In the golden rule of Jesus of Nazareth, we read the complete spirit of the ethics of utility. To do as you would be done by, and to love your neighbour as yourself, constitute the ideal perfection of utilitarian morality.' Against such claims we drew attention to the way in which love is concerned with the *particular* situations of individuals and the obligations which arise towards them as a result of our particular relations to them. It is now time to expose more systematically the heart of the contrast between Christian love and the purely computative, consequentialist type of approach which we observed in the previous chapter.

Newman, in a sermon for the Feast of St John the Evangelist, presents the Catholic position with admirable clarity. After remarking that it has ever been 'the plan of Divine Providence to ground what is good and true in religion and morals, on the basis of our good natural feelings', he goes on to draw certain inferences:

It is obviously impossible to love all men in any strict

and true sense. What is meant by loving all men is, to feel well-disposed to all men, to be ready to assist them, and to act towards those who come in our way, as if we loved them. . . . And love, besides, is a habit, and cannot be attained without actual practice, which on so large a scale is impossible. We see then how absurd it is when writers (as in the manner of some who slight the Gospel) talk magnificently about loving the whole human race with a comprehensive affection, of being the friends of all mankind, and the like. Such vaunting professions, what do they come to? that such men have certain benevolent feelings towards the world, — feelings and nothing more; — nothing more than unstable feelings, the mere offspring of an indulged imagination, which exists only when their minds are wrought upon, and are sure to fail them in the hour of need. This is not to love men, it is but to talk about love. — The real love of man must depend on practice, and therefore, must begin by exercising itself on our friends around us, otherwise it will have no existence. By trying to love our relations and friends, by submitting to their wishes, though contrary to our own, by bearing with their infirmities, by overcoming their occasional waywardness by kindness, by dwelling on their excellences, and trying to copy them, thus it is that we form in our hearts that root of charity which, though small at first, may, like the mustard seed, at last even overshadow the earth. (*Parochial and Plain Sermons*, vol. II, pp. 54—5)

The sermon in fact opens by pointing out that even God Incarnate was partial in his love in that St John is known as 'the disciple whom Jesus loved' (John 13:23), and so, in paying more attention to some rather than others, there can be for the Christian 'nothing inconsistent with the fulness of Christian love'. This is confirmed by Christ's life in general and by the particular way in which he introduces the commandment to love. Thus, it certainly cannot be claimed that Christ acted in the best utilitarian way in his life on earth, in the sense that he tried to achieve the maximum good of which he was capable. For, quantitatively, he could probably have achieved far more by being in an influential position on the staff of Pontius Pilate or Herod. Again there is no record of him seeking out the sick and healing as many of them as he possibly could. All that can be said is that with each individual he encountered and entered into some sort of relationship, he saw that particular person's need and met it. Equally, when one considers the interpretation of the term 'neighbour', in the command to love our neighbour as ourself, which Christ gives in his parable of the Good Samaritan (Luke 10:25ff), one finds no demand for generalized, impartial benevolence. The Good Samaritan acts only for the benefit of the one wounded traveller he encountered. He does not, for instance, set up a fund to help other travellers suffering similar misfortunes on the road. So, strictly speaking, the parable justifies the inference, not that one's neighbour is anyone, but rather anyone in need whom one personally encounters or with whom one enters into some sort of relation. This is not to deny the challenge for love to become more extensive in its concerns. It is simply to point out that, according to Jesus, the failure of love is at its most fundamental only where personal encounter or responsibility is involved. V. P. Furnish in his work, *The Love Command in the New Testament*, endorses this interpretation, quoting Bultmann in support: 'Bultmann rightly sees that the love command does not demand general love of man . . . based on an abstract or ideal value of man, but love of the real man, with whom I am bound up, based on nothing but the fact that he is my neighbour, whom I understand as such only in loving.'

Such is the all but unanimous voice of the Catholic tradition. Admittedly, Augustine seems to have preferred a universalist, impartial interpretation, but in this he is an exception within the early Church. From the time of Thomas Aquinas onwards there is no doubt that both the psychological and moral necessity of realizing that love is a relation to *specific* individuals is fully taken into account.

Aquinas himself does not hesitate to underline the fact that, the greater the number of connections we have with another person, the more love can and ought to bind us to them:

> We love them more because we love them in more ways. For those who are not connected with us are loved only with the friendship of charity, but towards those connected with us, other kinds of friendship come into play, dictated by the kind of tie that binds us together . . . So, to love someone because he is a kinsman, or connected to us, or is a fellow citizen, or because of any other lawful reason that accords with the end of charity, is an act that can be commanded by charity. (*Summa Theologiae*, 2a, 2ae, 26, 7)

Likewise, Bishop Butler protests against the equation of love, and indeed of all virtue, with a generalized benevolence. He suggests that, even if God is a utilitarian, he has so made our nature that we must not be.

> The fact then appears to be, that we are so constituted so as to condemn falsehood, unprovoked violence, injustice, and to approve benevolence to some preferably to others, abstracted from all consideration, which conduct is likeliest to produce an overbalance of happiness or misery. And therefore, were the Author of Nature to propose nothing to himself as an end but the production of happiness, were his moral character merely that of benevolence; yet ours is not so. Upon that supposition indeed the only reason of his giving us the above-mentioned approbation of benevolence to some persons rather than others, and disapprobation of falsehood, unprovoked violence, and injustice, must be that he foresaw this constitution of our nature would produce more happiness, than forming us with a temper of more general benevolence. (*Fifteen Sermons*, p. 152)

As a final illustration, one might note the words of Henry

Peschke in his *Christian Ethics*, the most easily readable of contemporary Roman Catholic surveys. After remarking that 'Christ extends the commandment of fraternal love to every man', he goes on to note that 'in concrete, the neighbour to be loved is everyone who by God's providential disposition is brought near to the Christian in order that he should serve and help him'.

Given such a framework, the psychological reason why the Christian will place considerable emphasis on the sacredness of the individual person becomes readily explicable. The entire practice of his habit of love will have been geared towards seeing the unique worth of each individual who, as Newman puts it, 'comes in our way' or, as Peschke puts it, 'who by God's providential disposition is brought near in order that we should serve and help him'. That is very different from being in love with the notion of humanity as a whole. But it is not just a psychological fact that is being appealed to. Theological and moral reasons can also be given for this way of loving.

The moral reason is a further development of naturalism. God has made our natures for a purpose, and so true fulfilment for the person will only come through this kind of loving. On first hearing, this may sound like an extremely selfish version of Christianity, and indeed Protestant theologians, in order to avoid any suggestion of self-interest, often go so far as to claim that love of neighbour as self means instead of self. This is, for example, what Kierkegaard, Nygren and Reinhold Niebuhr do. But such an accusation can last only for so long as one fails to take account of the fact that it is a pre-condition of finding self-fulfilment or happiness in such conduct that one abandon any self-interested motive for so acting. If we may usurp Christ's words from a rather different context (Matt. 10:39), it is by losing one's life that one finds it. The point is that, though happiness may be the consequence of such conduct, the motive must be love of each and every individual for their own sake, not as a means to that happiness. It is also a point that applies with equal force to love of God. He must be loved for his own sake, not just as a means of getting to heaven. This is why there is no incongruity in all those passages about reward in the gospels, such as 'Blessed are ye when men shall ... persecute you ... for my sake ... for great is your reward in heaven' (Matt. 5:11—12). The reward is to follow as a consequence, and indeed if it were the individual's motive this would be to preclude the possibility of such a reward, because the action would not have been done out of love for God for his own sake. The true nature of the Christian ideal is expressed in St Francis Xavier's hymn:

> My God, I love thee; not because
> I hope for heaven thereby,
> Nor yet because who love thee not
> Are lost eternally.
>
> Thou, O my Jesus, thou didst me
> Upon the Cross embrace;
> For me didst bear the nails and spear,
> And manifold disgrace, ...
>
> Then why, O blessèd Jesus Christ,
> Should I not love thee well,
> Not for the sake of winning heaven,
> Or of escaping hell;
>
> Not with the hope of gaining aught,
> Not seeking a reward;
> But as thyself hast lovèd me,
> O ever-loving Lord?

The theological reason for seeing each individual as having a unique worth is grounded in the link between the first and second great commandments, love of God and love of neighbour. God is necessarily seen as being loved for what he already is, whereas human beings, even if they have no actual qualities that would evoke love, are none-theless seen as always worthy of love, in virtue of the potential each has been given by God. This potential is variously described. Aquinas, for example, says that even grave sinners must be loved, because they, like us, are 'capable of eternal happiness'. In such a case the natural disposition will have greatest difficulty in showing concern, in sympathizing with those whose actions threaten us. But there is no doubt that the Christian is called to such concern. 'Love your enemies . . . do good to them that hate you' (Matt. 5:44). A monster like Hitler thus remains an object of the Christian's love, because he continues to have the potential to be a very different kind of being. But the Scriptures also give an additional motive, the motive of gratitude — 'forgiving one another . . . even as Christ forgave you' (Col. 3:13).

If the Christian regards each individual person as sacred, with 'this world and all that is in it, as a mere shadow, as dust and ashes, compared with the value of one single soul' (as Newman said), it follows that it must take this individuality seriously. It was an inference that the Oxford Movement was not slow to draw. In a letter to his wife, Pusey wrote: 'It seems to me a main and very extensive error of the school to which he belongs [he is talking of an Evangelical] to forget the extent of the natural varieties of conformation of the human mind, and to suppose that the object of Christianity is rather to produce one uniform result, than to modify, chasten, exalt and sanctify the peculiar character of each . . . In the moral as well as the natural frame, what is healthful and nutritious to one person may be deadly poison to another.'

Isaac Williams in Tract 80, *On Reserve in Communicating Religious Knowledge*, has a brief section in which he applies the principle to the moral sphere by suggesting that stages in moral development should be recognized. He declares it acceptable that a person begin by pursuing good simply in order to win the praise of men. For 'it is a step, as it were, in the scale of virtue, that leads us, by human means, to the footstool of God'. The other example he gives is the way in which envy may initially be the spur to a more honourable form of emulation. This 'principle of reserve' seems to me to contain a useful insight that can be applied more widely. Very often, the only realistic approach to a particular situation is to act, or encourage others to act, with less than perfect motives in the hope that eventually the perfect may supervene. Indeed, arguably, this is the whole basis upon which the moral education of children is founded. Rewards and punishments only slowly give place to the acquisition of moral sensibilities. At all events, it is a principle to which I shall resort in subsequent chapters. It should be noted, however, that it is not an admission of the inevitability of sin, as with Luther, nor the advocacy of 'compromise' that one finds in the Roman Catholic moralist, Charles Curran. For it is seen as an essentially transitional phase, even if the transition may on occasion take many years to come about.

But it is love of God which remains the Christian's highest calling. In that love one loves the only being who possesses by right that eternal happiness which he offers to share with us. In such love we become, as St Thomas puts it following St John (15:14), the friends of God, and we delight to be in the presence of him whose love knows no bounds.

JUSTICE AND THE DIVINE SOCIETY

Here we come to one of the great inadequacies of the Oxford Movement. For it cannot be claimed that justice or indeed social issues played any great part in its thought. Admittedly, Keble was known for his kindly attitude to poor country folk, and Pusey once preached a university sermon on 'Almsgiving' in which he drew from the story of Dives and Lazarus (Luke 16:19ff) the following contemporary moral: 'A reckless, fraudful competition, whose aim is to cheapen every luxury and vanity in order that those at ease may spend on fresh accumulated luxuries and vanities what they withhold from the poor, lowers the price of things we crave for by cutting down the wages of the poor.' But, apart from that, one is already floundering. The only real exception at the intellectual level was W. G. Ward who, in *The Ideal of a Christian Church*, berated the rich for their oppression of the poor and indeed contemplated the study of political economy so that 'we can really and permanently benefit the poor'.

Properly speaking, it was only at a much later stage that the Catholic Movement in the Church of England became acutely aware of the social implications of Christian ethics. In 1877 the Guild of St Matthew was founded, among whose members was numbered Thomas Hancock, Father Stanton and the colourful Stewart Headlam who, according to another member, James Adderley, based his position on the view that 'the Mass was the weekly meeting of a society of rebels against a Mammon-worshipping world order'. Then in 1899 the Christian Social Union was created, a much more intellectually based society, whose leading influences were Charles Gore and Henry Scott Holland. In the 1920s, taking a lead from Gore, this was succeeded by the Christendom Group, with Maurice Reckitt and V. A. Demant and their summer schools of Christian sociology. More recently, the Jubilee Group has been formed.

Whether such reflection has always been wise or clearly thought-out is a secondary matter. What is vital is that the appropriateness of such reflection within the Catholic moral tradition should be acknowledged. Before outlining the reasons for this, some indication must be given as to why it was historically a not unnatural grafting onto the traditions of the Oxford Movement. There appear to have been two major influences, one implicit in Tractarianism, the other stemming from F. D. Maurice. W. G. Peck, one of the members of the Christendom Group, observed that the Assize Sermon with which Keble began the Movement in 1833 has, despite surface appearances, profound implications. In *The Social Implications of the Oxford Movement* he noted that, while at one level it was merely a protest about the suppression of some Irish bishoprics by the government of the day, 'it was a claim of yet deeper import. It was the implicit enunciation of a Divine Society independent of the secular power: an order built upon the Incarnation of the Son of God, which must derive its principle of cohesion from supernatural forces and must therefore be capable of rebuking the order established in the world.' At all events, this seemed to later followers of the Movement the all but inevitable inference to draw, especially given the Tractarian emphasis on the objective character of the sacraments, as means of grace not under the control of men. But there was also a more explicit, intellectual force at work, the thought of F. D. Maurice. When his book, *The Kingdom of Christ*, first came out in 1838, many reviewers identified him as a Tractarian sympathizer. Although this turned out not to be the case, the Catholic ideas present undoubtedly had a profound influence on subsequent thought.

If the reader is puzzled about how one can claim this to be a central plank in Catholic moral theology and yet admit its absence in the Tractarians, one should recall that the same phenomenon occurred in contemporary Rome. Under Pius IX (1846—78) the papacy exhibited positive hostility to change in the social order, and a more balanced view was only obtained with Leo XIII and his successors.

But, enough of history. The reasons why this has been made, and must continue to be made, a central plank in the Catholic position are fourfold — biblical, analytical, naturalist and sacramental. The first two have already been referred to, when discussing Liberation theology in the first chapter. There is no need to remind the reader again of the wealth of biblical, especially Old Testament texts, on the subject. By 'analytical' we simply mean the fact that an analysis of love shows the necessity for acting justly. We cannot claim to be loving someone at the same time as we fail to give him his due, what is his by right. Aquinas brings out the point well by also making it part of a contrast between loving God and our more basic duty of serving him. 'As loving our neighbour is included in loving God, so rendering each his due is comprised in serving him.' The naturalist and sacramental reasons correspond to the two main influences on the later phases of the Catholic movement in the Church of England, and to these we now turn.

The naturalist reason was Maurice's contribution, though it is far older than him. *The Kingdom of Christ* resonates with the oft-repeated theme of human beings as essentially social beings. For Maurice, it is a fact of nature which exists on three levels, family, state and Church. Of the family he writes: 'The family order and constitution is the first great bulwark which God has provided against the dominion of the senses and of the outward world . . . it is the great influence which redeems the affections from things, and gives them a direction towards persons — it is the commencement of all society — it is the first step towards the acknowledgement of God.' Of the other two, he remarks a couple of pages later: 'In a state I say everyone must dwell not only for purposes of safety and protection but in order that his moral and spiritual being may be properly developed. Such a state, I say, is as much implied in the constitution of man as a Church is implied in that constitution; such a state is as much a witness for God in one way as a Church is a witness for him in another way.' The state is thus charged with looking after the external man, the Church with the internal. But, since both are religious institutions, the Church is entitled to keep an oversight of the workings of the state. The claim that questions of justice are unavoidable, because God has made man for social relations and interdependence, had already been fully endorsed by Aquinas centuries earlier. He insisted that it has nothing to do with the Fall. 'Man is a naturally social animal; men even in the state of innocence would have lived in society.' Maurice, the erstwhile Unitarian, in one of his essays, 'The Trinity in Unity', even argues that we should think of God as a social being. But, given the Catholic emphasis on the sacredness of the person and the constant danger to which this is exposed of being confused with the modern cult of individualism, perhaps Maurice's most useful comment occurs in a letter to R. C. Trench: 'I am more and more convinced that we must not use "personal" and "individual" as synonymous words; but that, in fact, we shall have most sense and lively realisation of our distinct personality when we cease to be individuals, and most delight to contemplate ourselves as members of one body in one Head.'

The other reason, the sacramental, can perhaps best be elucidated by asking the reader to reflect on the scriptural use of the term, the Body of Christ. For, not only does Christ become present in the Eucharist (1 Cor. 11:29), we become his body by being incorporated into him as his members (1 Cor. 12:27; Eph. 1:23). Add to that the image of the vine and its branches in St John (chapter 15). What then emerges as we celebrate the Eucharist is a constant reminder not only of our dependence on Christ but of our dependence on one another. 'The eye cannot say to the hand, "I do not need you"; nor the head to the feet, "I do not need you." Quite the contrary: those organs of the body which seem to be more frail than others are indispensable . . . If one organ suffers, they all suffer together. If one flourishes, they all rejoice together' (I Cor. 12:21ff – NEB). Simply because of the ramifications of this image and the indissoluble link with the sacrament, the Catholic cannot fail to be reminded each time he takes Communion of the need for social justice, of the need for the relations between the different members to be as is their due.

Let me end with two cautionary comments. First, care must be taken in distinguishing demands of love and demands of justice. A community based on love is, of course, the Christian's ideal. But love can never be forced, and so justice must remain one's first, more basic objective. It is a distinction Christians do not always observe. Yet there is a fundamental difference between what someone is entitled to as of right and what it would merely be good to do for him. Failure to observe the distinction will inevitably make the Church's pronouncements on social injustice less effective. They will be read as the usual high expectations of Christian love, rather than as root and branch condemnation of something fundamentally wrong with a society.

A second way in which Catholic moral theology will become less effective is if it confuses means and ends. Christian ethics is certainly concerned with the self-realization of men in community, with the realization of a happiness that will anticipate the perfect happiness that can be theirs in heaven. But the means can often be confused with the end, and the assumption made that there is only one way towards the achievement of the ideal, whether it be the politics of left or right. Certainly, the individual Christian must think about the means. Certainly, too, sometimes there is in fact only one way. But individual Christians will only do the voice of the Church harm if they insist on it normally publicly identifying with one particular approach. History is littered with examples of this lack of realism.

Yet, on the other side, Christianity has sometimes failed to endorse at the time what it has seen in retrospect to have been a basic demand of justice. One area where such problems occur in a particularly acute form is the question of the ethics of work. It is to that which I therefore turn as the first area of specific moral dilemma for investigation.

FURTHER READING

On natural law and conscience

J. H. Newman, *University Sermons* (No. 2) (ed. D. M. MacKinnon and J. D. Holmes), SPCK, 1970

Joseph Butler, *Fifteen Sermons Preached at the Rolls Chapel* (Nos. 1–3) (ed. T. A. Roberts), SPCK, 1970

On formation and growth in holiness

J. H. Newman, *University Sermons* (No. 3)

Dante, *The Divine Comedy* (Part 2, 'Purgatory', deals with the seven deadly sins.) trans. J. D. Sinclair O.U.P., 1961

P. T. Geach, *The Virtues*, Cambridge University Press, 1977 (by a philosopher)

On love and the sacredness of the person

J. H. Newman, *Parochial and Plain Sermons*, vol. 2 (No. 5), Rivingtons, 1868 (not easily accessible)

Joseph Butler, *Fifteen Sermons* (Nos. 11–14)

On justice and the divine society

F. D. Maurice, *Theological Essays* (Nos. 15 and 16 on Church and Trinity), J. Clark, 1957 (most easily accessible relevant work of Maurice)

3   Choices at Work

Given that work is man's central activity, one might have thought that more Christian moral reflection would have been directed here than at any other point. But this is very far from being the case. The explanation lies in the Church's failure to adapt to change in all its ramifications — the possibility of it, the fact of it and the moral necessity for it.

Thus, while in the Old Testament there are denunciations of serious social injustice, one's lot, whether of poverty or riches, is normally seen as ordered by the hand of God (e.g. Pss. 112:3 and 1.3), and no thought is given to a major re-shaping of society. At the time it was probably not a live option, but, unfortunately, the influence of such passages continued long after this had changed. Adam Smith saw in his free trade economics the invisible hand of divine justice, and it is a view reflected in the writings of many less famous men. A Puritan tract of 1654 (R. Younge's 'The Poores' Advocate') maintains that there is 'no question but riches should be the portion of the godly than of the wicked, were it good for them. For godliness hath the promises of this life as well as the life to come'. Again, one of America's most distinguished preachers of the nineteenth century, Henry Ward Beecher, could declare: 'Looking comprehensively through city and town and village and country, the general truth will stand, that no man in this land suffers from poverty unless it be more than his fault — unless it be his sin.'

But it was not just the failure to consider the possibility of engineered change as compatible with divine providence that worked against Christian reflection. The fact of change itself also caused problems. The only period when sustained reflection was given to such issues was, as we shall see, the Middle Ages; but this reflection failed to adapt to the major change of the coming of capitalism.

Finally, it is only in modern times that Christians have begun to appreciate the extent to which one man may be causally responsible for the lot of another, whether through conditions of employment, government policy or conditions of trade.

However, the trend is being reversed. Particularly impressive are the series of papal encyclicals that began with Leo XIII's *Rerum Novarum* of 1891 (often referred to as 'the Worker's Charter'), followed by Pius XI's *Quadragesimo Anno* in 1931 and John XXIII's *Mater et Magistra* in 1961, and most recently by John Paul II's *Laborem Exercens* in 1981. Even so, it is still probably the most neglected area of Christian ethics. That is a pity. For the Christian should be prepared to face the modern world. Even if he cannot normally find specific injunctions from the Bible to apply to that world, there are always available general Catholic principles of the kind referred to in the previous chapter. It is to the application of these principles that we now turn.

THE RIGHT TO MEANINGFUL WORK

The Bible acknowledges that work was part of God's original plan of creation (Gen. 2:15), though it sees its conditions having been affected by the Fall (Gen. 3:19). However, it is a matter to which no great thought is given. There is only one extended discussion, in the Apocryphal book of Ecclesiasticus, where scholar and craftsman are contrasted to the latter's disadvantage, though the indispensability of his role is admitted (38:24—39). The absence of any sustained reflection admits of a ready explanation. In such a primitive agrarian society there was little, if any, freedom of manoeuvre. 'Man goeth forth unto his work and to his labour until the evening' (Ps. 104:23).

But all that changed with the Industrial Revolution. Man gained greater freedom with his ability to sell his labour where he would, but this was more than offset by the horrendous conditions of much employment. Child labour, long hours and so forth have long since disappeared, at least from the developed world, but this is not to say that the question of meaning in work has been satisfactorily resolved. The craftsman or farm worker can gain satisfaction from the significance he sees in his work in a way that, through automation and other factors, is often denied to the factory worker. It was a point Marx and Engels drew attention to in 1848 in their *Communist Manifesto*: 'Owing to the extensive use of machinery and to division of labour, the work of the proletarians has lost all individual character, and, consequently, all charm for the workman. He becomes an appendage of the machine, and it is only the most simple, the most monotonous, and most easily acquired knack that is required of him.' An illustration of this would be the River Rouge Works of Ford, which are more than twenty-six miles long and require forty-five operations for assembling the chassis, each one being performed by a different worker. As examples from England, one might mention current problems on the railways and in the newspaper industry. For the argument concerns, not just staffing levels, but the ultimate disappearance of the engine drivers' union (a process that began with the disappearance of steam) and in Fleet Street the reduction of skills required as newspapers move over from traditional letterpress printing to lithographic processes. But it is not just automation that raises questions of meaning. These are also raised by what Marx calls the division of labour − the feeling of insignificance an individual may have in large factories, the feeling of being a mere cog in a vast machine.

That a Catholic must be concerned with such issues is an implication of his naturalist assumptions. Morality is as much concerned with fulfilment at work as it is with fulfilment in other aspects of life. It is therefore a just expectation on the part of a worker that his employer should make his conditions of employment as fulfiling as is reasonably possible. Pope John was in no doubt about this when he produced *Mater et Magistra*:

Justice is to be observed not only in the distribution of wealth, but also in regard to the conditions in which men are engaged in producing this wealth. Every man has, of his very nature, a need to express himself in his work and thereby to perfect his own being. Consequently, if the whole structure and organization of an economic system is such as to compromise human dignity, to lessen a man's sense of responsibility or rob him of any opportunity for exercising personal initiative, then such a system, we maintain, is altogether unjust — no matter how much wealth it produces, or how justly and equitably such wealth is distributed . (82–3)

But, it may be said, the Pope exaggerates the importance of such questions to human fulfilment. Henry Ford once remarked that 'the average worker . . . wants a job in which he doesn't have to think', and it is possible to produce some empirical evidence in his support. J. Goldthorpe, basing his conclusions on research in Luton, maintains (in *The Affluent Worker*) that the worker is generally content. And at the managerial level W. H. Whyte, in his classic study *The Organisation Man*, found executives content to have their personalities chiselled to fit the needs of their particular corporation. From there it might be but a short step to endorsement of the views of Frederick Taylor (1856–1915), the American father of 'scientific management', who conceived the relation between management and worker as that between a planner desiring maximum production and a machine. But this would be the wrong inference to make. Rationalization on Taylorian principles was soon seen to be counter-productive, as is illustrated by what happened at an American factory of the Worthington Pump Corporation, where such principles were applied but resulted, between 1926 and 1929, in an increase from 12 per cent to 34 per cent in those absent from work through nervous depression. Equally, though Goldthorpe found workers content, it was only in the limited sense of seeing their work as successfully instrumental in achieving the means for the enjoyment of pleasure outside working hours. Finally, even when contentment does seem to be produced, as with Whyte's 'organization man', one is still appalled at the limited nature of such contentment, as indeed Whyte was, preferring instead what he calls 'individualism within organization life'.

In fact the evidence is so overwhelmingly in favour of Pope John's view, that it is now clear that even paternalism is no adequate substitute for scientific management. Thus, in a comment still relevant today, J. A. C. Brown saw the major issue facing mid-twentieth-century industry in the fact that, although managers have in general advanced beyond the stage of treating the worker as just a machine, they have not sufficiently progressed to realize that being an individual he needs to be treated as a *responsible* human being.

> No self-respecting individual wishes to be treated like a child, or a cow in a model dairy — if he is offered something for nothing he will, of course, take it but he will not like the purveyor of goods any better. A worker in the Michelin factories in France, which are noted for their social schemes, expressed himself thus concerning their welfare: I was born into Michelin baby linen and fed with a Michelin bottle in a Michelin house . . . If I don't get out of this joint directly, I shall soon be buried in a Michelin coffin. (*The Social Psychology of Industry*, p. 278)

It is an impression confirmed by the well-known Jewish industrial psychologist, Frederick Herzberg. In his book, *Work and the Nature of Man*, following the rather dubious lead given by the eleventh-century commentator, Rashi, he takes the picture of Adam in Genesis 2 to be of man as feeble-minded and essentially concerned with the avoidance of pain, while the image of Abraham in Genesis 17 he takes to be a positive one, concerned with the fulfilment of man's potential. He then develops this picture in terms of two basic types of needs, the Adamic and the Abrahamic, the former being concerned with protection against hunger, the need for shelter, etc., and the latter with one's need for achievement, recognition, etc. The main thrust of his argument is that the profit motive is really only an incentive to Adam, and that industry ignores the Abrahamic side of man at its peril. Later in the book he explains why he describes those aspects of work relating to the Adam in man as hygiene factors, and those relating to Abraham as motivation factors. This is because satisfaction of the needs of Adam, while preventing job dissatisfaction, does little to create positive job attitudes, whereas fulfilment of the needs of Abraham is effective in motivating the individual to superior performance and effort. The main factors affecting the Adam in man are listed as company policy and administration, supervision, relation with other workers and work conditions, while those affecting the Abraham include achievement, recognition, the work itself and responsibility. Two whole chapters are devoted to offering an impressive array of empirical evidence, including some from the Soviet Union, in support of his theory.

The reader may have found this excursion into industrial psychology somewhat surprising. But he must remember that Catholic moral theology, in assuming that the fulfilment of human nature is a good thing, is under an obligation to check what is in fact necessary towards that fulfilment. It is therefore particularly satisfying to find industrial psychologists in effect endorsing current trends in papal teaching. But, if the objectives are clear in requiring greater opportunities for a sense of pride and responsibility in one's work, the next question that arises is the means towards this end. Here too the papacy has not been slow in making suggestions. In a passage that almost anticipates Schumacher's best-seller, *Small is Beautiful*, Pius XI declares in *Quadragesimo Anno* that 'just as it is wrong to withdraw from the individual and commit to a group what private enterprise and industry can accomplish, so too it is an injustice, a grave evil and a disturbance of right order, for a larger and higher association to arrogate to itself functions which can be performed efficiently by smaller and lower societies'. Again, John XXIII is emphatic that 'we are in no two minds as to the need for giving workers an active share in the business of the company for which they work — be it a private or a public one.' Both were at the time misinterpreted as making very specific recommendations, Pius XI as supporting Mussolini's policy of trying to build up a state-controlled corporative system, John XXIII as advocating that workers should be allocated shares in the firms for which they work. In the latter case it was due to a mistranslation of the Latin; the Pope in fact declared in the next sentence that 'it is not, of course, possible to lay down hard and fast rules regarding the manner of such participation'. But, despite the understandable papal caution, it is essential to consider how these two demands might be implemented, if any progress is to be made at all.

So far as Pius XI's suggestion of a reduction of scale is concerned, one might initially think that the trend has been entirely in the opposite direction, especially with the growth of multinational corporations. But even these seldom function as a single operation, given their tendency to diversify into a number of different products in order to achieve greater financial security. In addition, there are a number of hopeful experiments in the treatment of the factory assembly line. One method, first tried before the Second World War at the Bat'a shoe factory at Zlin in Moravia, is to treat each of the automated stages as if it were fully autonomous, allowing each stage to buy the materials from the previous stage and then sell their completed product to the next stage on, with incentive gains being offered for increased productivity. An alternative approach, popularized in Sweden, is to move the worker through the various stages so that he has some comprehension of the process as a whole, and so hopefully more identification with what is taking place.

Implementation of John XXIII's suggestion for greater worker involvement might assume a number of different patterns. One major British company, ICI, give their employees shares in the company. Under the last Labour government the notion of co-operatives run by the workers was experimented with, as, for instance, the Meriden motorcycle co-operative, but none flourished, largely because they involved the take-over of industries already in difficulty. The most commonly tried option is worker representation on company boards. In some western European countries (e.g. Sweden and West Germany) this is already compulsory. In Britain worker directors were introduced into the steel industry when it was renationalized in 1967 under Lord Melchett. In 1977 an official government committee under Lord Bullock recommended equal representation for trade unions and shareholders on the boards of Britain's top 735 companies with over 2,000 employees. They also favoured co-opted directors from outside the company, mutually agreed, and not exceeding a third of the total. This so-called 2X + Y formula would have given Britain a more radical system than anywhere else in Europe, but no action was taken. Whether one believes that greater participation should be confined to the task level, to there being a greater say for the individual over the organization of his labour, or that this should be extended to policy-making as well, one thing emerges clearly, given the Catholic emphasis on the sacredness of the person. As Fr Peter Mayhew puts it in *Justice in Industry*, written after visiting numerous factories throughout Britain: 'First and foremost, I must say quite plainly that there is a basic need in industry for both corporate structures and individual functions to be so arranged that the worker feels involved.' For without such involvement the treatment of the individual as a machine-making machine, a mere impersonal means, will be the inevitable result.

One last point needs underlining. If the right to meaningful work is a fundamental right of man, then the right to work itself is an even more basic right. John Paul II declares in *Laborem Exercens* that, even if the direct employer cannot continue to guarantee employment, there is an obligation on the indirect employer to endeavour to do so. By 'indirect employer' he means largely the government and the way in which it structures the economy. His view is that 'the role of the agents included under the title of indirect employer is to act against unemployment, which in all cases is an evil', its inherent evil deriving from the fact that 'man's life is built up every day from work, from work it derives its specific dignity'. No one can doubt this who speaks to the unemployed and realizes the effect of the judgement of society upon them in declaring their contribution useless or unwanted. Now, of course, a government may be unable to achieve full employment or it may argue, as the present governments of Britain and the United States do, that increased unemployment is the only way of bringing inflation under control. But, even if this is true, it can never be regarded morally as a permitted permanent solution. With such interim measures there will in any case, as John Paul says, be 'the obligation to provide unemployment benefits' since this is 'a duty springing from the fundamental principle of the moral order in this sphere, namely the principle of the common use of goods'. In other words, the way society is structured is a responsibility of the whole of that society. The natural order, the order intended by God, is not that which just happens by chance. The aim in the long term, as an act of basic justice, not charity, must thus be full employment, which presumably with the advent of the micro-chip will mean shorter working hours for us all and a sharing out of the work involved.

JUSTICE IN WAGES AND PROFITS

One of the saddest facts about the history of the Christian ethical tradition is that, prior to the advent of capitalism, reflection on the morality of wages and profits was flourishing, and then it all but died out until the present century. Even now discussion is seldom conducted at any great depth.

So far as the question of profits is concerned, there was a strong medieval ethical tradition against the practice of lending at interest. This had two sources, one biblical and

...hlin, whether this applied only to the worker or also ...is family, a reply came from the Vatican that one that ...ported the worker only might not be contrary to justice, ...igh it would be inconsistent with charity. But, by 1961 ...n XXIII was taking a much firmer line: 'We consider ...ur duty to reaffirm that the remuneration of work is ...something that can be left to the laws of the market; ...ought it to be fixed arbitrarily . . . which means that ...kers must be paid a wage which allows them to live a ...y human life and to fulfil their family obligations in a ...thy manner.' He then goes on to list other factors ...ch 'enter into the assessment of a just wage'. But no ...mpt is made to suggest how they might be balanced ...inst each other, nor is reference made to the most ...mon sources of complaint, comparative levels of pay ...between similar occupations and the maintenance of ...erentials. Even less is to be found on the question of ...w just profits might be determined.

...o far as the just wage is concerned, one must go back ...first principles, which is indeed what John Paul II urges ...to do. Wages, he points out, are the 'practical means ...ereby the vast majority of people can have access to ...se goods which are intended for common use' and so ...just wage is the concrete means of verifying the justice ...the whole socioeconomic system'. In other words, he is ...ling us back to the Thomist principle that the division ...goods is secondary to the basic naturalist demand that, ...wever society is structured, it must be such that the ...lividual is able to fulfil the potential which God has ...en him. The right to meaningful work and the right to ...adequate wage are thus part and parcel of the same ...turalist assumption.

...Papal encyclicals do not clearly distinguish between a ...st wage in the sense of an adequate minimum wage and ...fair wage, comparative to other workers. It is to the ...ter issue that we must now turn. Many Christians these ...ys might be tempted to quote Marx, 'from each accord-...g to his ability, to each according to his needs', and argue ...at this is the strategy most compatible with the demands

one from natural law. Thus, there are numerous Old Testament passages which condemn the practice of usury, for example Exodus 22:25, Deuteronomy 23:20 and Psalm 5. (It should, incidentally, be noted that the Authorized Version translation 'usury' refers to the taking of any interest at all, not as in modern English to the taking of exorbitant profit.) The motive for the biblical prohibition was probably primarily one of compassion (cf. Ezek. 22:12). We have evidence from Upper Mesopotamia that interest on money loans was sometimes as much as 50 per cent. But in the medieval period the natural-law argument with its appeal to the 'barren' nature of money certainly also played its part. Aristotle had argued in the *Politics* that 'very much disliked is the practice of charging interest; and the dislike is fully justified. For interest is a yield arising out of money itself, not a product of that for which money was provided . . . Hence of all ways of getting wealth this is the most contrary to nature.' At its simplest, the moral objection is that one is getting something for doing nothing. There is no wear and tear on money; in itself it produces nothing; it is a mere barren means of exchange. It was an argument fully endorsed by Aquinas, though it is important to note its wider setting. His view is that 'private property is not opposed to natural law, but is an addition to it, devised by human reason,' a necessary institution in a fallen world, since men work more and dispute less when goods are private. The result is that he sees no wrong in theft, when something is taken for necessary sustenance, and this probably also explains his reluctance to admit that any increase in one's private property could be justified, except what one has achieved by one's personal labour. That is to say, property is seen as a secondary institution for a fallen world, and so in difficult cases — for example, hunger or an attempt to increase one's property — one must fall back on more basic naturalist principles. However that may be, later medieval thinkers, such as Duns Scotus (died 1308) and still more so St Antoninus, Archbishop of Florence (1389—1459), were prepared to argue the lender's case by drawing attention to such factors as the labour and risk involved and the legitimacy of the trader attempting to preserve his present standard of living. But these early attempts to come to terms with the rise of capitalism were not pursued. At the Reformation, on the Protestant side Luther showed no sympathy with what he saw as the corrupting spirit of commerce, and he held up the life of the peasant as the ideal since this was furthest removed from the influence of commerce. Equally Calvin, while more tolerant of trade and accepting the morality of interest, showed no inclination to pursue the ethical issues in any of the detail to be observed in Antoninus' *Summa Theologica Moralis*. But, to be fair, the Counter-Reformation showed no more willingness to come to terms with the modern world; Benedict XIV issued papal condemnations of usury as late as the mid-eighteenth century.

Unfortunately, the history of Christian reflection on what might constitute a just wage is equally depressing. Once again, St Antoninus played a leading role, with his theories being popularized by his contemporary, the Franciscan, St Bernardino of Siena. His reflections were then followed up in the sixteenth and seventeenth centuries by Molina, Lessius and de Lugo. Fogarty in an appendix to his book, *The Just Wage*, usefully summarizes their suggested principles under four headings. First, there is equal pay for equal working capacity, by which is meant that reference should be made to conditions in the labour market as a whole without regard to artificial conditions such as the existence of a local monopoly. Secondly, account must be taken of the common good, of the welfare of the community as a whole, including special obligations to one's family and the poor. Henry of Langenstein, Vice-Chancellor of the University of Paris in the fourteenth century, is in no doubt that this will require a highly controlled economy. Both these principles would be accepted as having continued relevance today. The other two are more contentious, and indicate the inherently conservative nature of their thought, despite their acceptance of a planned economy. Thirdly, there must be avoidance of compensation between conditions. That is to say,

rank, prestige and wealth should go togethe[r]
to give this condition a charitable interp[retation as]
Lugo did, by pointing out that a break[down]
through bad working conditions is not com[pensated by]
increased wages; the objective should rathe[r]
of the bad conditions. But, in general, th[is was]
interpreted by the fourth, to each accordi[ng]
or, as Antoninus put it, 'that the person co[ncerned is]
able to manage and provide for himself and[]
ing to his status'. Lessius in fact uses this a[s]
for taxation, inasmuch as one can see its[]
being in order to 'maintain the dignity of[]
for the labourer is worthy of his hire'. Yet[]
should note that there was also a compassion[ate]
principle. For it was in effect a plea for grea[ter]
wages so that, for instance, a craftsman sho[uld]
sudden poverty nor insufficient resources to[]
of his trade. Equally, status was not thoug[ht]
bringing privileges but also social obligations[]
reminds the nobility that their status bring[s]
duty of service to the community, and it w[as]
theme in the popular preaching of St Berna[rdino]
was a responsible conservatism. One might a[dd]
one would be hard put to it to name a single c[]
moral theologian who has devoted an entire[]
ethics of economics in the way Lessius di[d in]
Justitia et Jure. The explanation for the decli[ne of]
reflection here is more difficult to identify, b[ut]
it was due to the conservatism of the theory a[nd diffi]
culty of adapting it to the more fluid socie[ty]
emerging. No one had the imagination or cour[age to]
again the attempt to apply Catholic principles[]
social situation.

Certainly, papal encyclicals operate at a mu[ch more pro]
found level on this issue than was the case with t[]
of the meaning of work. Still, progress is being[]
XIII merely demanded 'that wages ought not t[o be insuf]
ficient to support a frugal and well-behaved wa[]
Indeed, when pressed by Cardinal Gossens, Arc[h]

66

67

of love. Certainly, it would be odd if a family failed to abide by this principle. But this does not mean that it is a basic demand of justice, what a person is entitled to as of right, which is how questions of social policy should be determined where an element of compulsion is involved. As we have seen, it is of course true that a person is entitled to expect his society to ensure a minimum wage for him, sufficient to provide the means whereby he is able to realize his self-potential through satisfaction of his basic needs. But there is a vast range of wants and desires beyond this point, the satisfaction of which, though reasonable in itself, cannot be regarded as a prerequisite to the possibility of such self-fulfilment — for example, a large garden or world travel.

That being so, some other principle must be employed. None is likely to be entirely fair. Indeed, it would be dangerous if a perfectly fair system could be devised, dangerous both economically and theologically: economically because there would not then be sufficient flexibility to ensure job mobility as the economy required it; theologically because there would then be a strong temptation to identify personal worth with material worth. But this is not to say that no improvements can be made. My own view is that, the more inherited advantages are discounted, whether these be genetic (e.g. intelligence) or legal (e.g. wealth), the fairer the system. Greater emphasis can then be placed on rewarding what depends most on the individual himself, his own efforts and increased responsibility that may accrue to him as a result. Both criteria can be criticized; effort because what may be easy for one man may be exceedingly hard for another, responsibility because power can bring its own compensations. But such difficulties should not be exaggerated. In practice, rough estimates of an individual's actual efforts as compared with his potential are already being made, for example, in productivity schemes. As for responsibility, provided in the individual's chosen occupation there is equality of opportunity to reach the top, it is surely fair to reward the effort expended in terms of training etc. that has led him to secure such a position, as well as the greater efforts that may now be expected of him. If it is objected that effort is also not under a person's control but conditioned early, this seems to me false, and in any case incompatible with the Christian emphasis on personal responsibility, that one is capable of change.

As a matter of fact, even Marxist societies have found it necessary to maintain differentials. In 1963 a Peking journal declared that 'even if pay according to work is bourgeois, it helps socialist reconstruction', while forty years earlier in 1921 Lenin saw his immediate aim in similar terms: 'Not directly relying on enthusiasm, but . . . on the basis of personal interest, personal incentive and business principles, we . . . must set to work'. That this is also what happens in practice is confirmed by Sir Henry Phelps Brown in his book, *The Inequality of Pay*, which is a major comparative study of wage differences in Britain, western and eastern Europe and North America. Particularly interesting to note is that in general he found the same differential ordering of occupations throughout. The only difference was a narrower gap between top and bottom in Soviet economies, though even here there were exceptions; in 1956 in one Russian iron and steel plant the top manager was getting twenty times the wage of the lowest paid manual worker. Some empirical research also suggests that such differentials correspond to what is felt by the workers themselves to be fair. Elliott Jaques for instance, as a result of investigating the views of over 3,000 employees in various industries, came to the conclusion that wages were felt to be fair in so far as they reflected a measurement of the differing 'time span of discretion' involved, i.e. the maximum time lapse over which a person is required to exercise discretion in his job without that discretion being reviewed (labourer up to a day, clerk up to a week, foreman up to a year, general manager up to five years). Though his proposals have been accepted in a number of companies in Britain, the United States and the Netherlands, they have been criticized for failing to take account of other factors such as skill, experience, training and qualifications, though

70

one from natural law. Thus, there are numerous Old Testament passages which condemn the practice of usury, for example Exodus 22:25, Deuteronomy 23:20 and Psalm 5. (It should, incidentally, be noted that the Authorized Version translation 'usury' refers to the taking of any interest at all, not as in modern English to the taking of exorbitant profit.) The motive for the biblical prohibition was probably primarily one of compassion (cf. Ezek. 22:12). We have evidence from Upper Mesopotamia that interest on money loans was sometimes as much as 50 per cent. But in the medieval period the natural-law argument with its appeal to the 'barren' nature of money certainly also played its part. Aristotle had argued in the *Politics* that 'very much disliked is the practice of charging interest; and the dislike is fully justified. For interest is a yield arising out of money itself, not a product of that for which money was provided . . . Hence of all ways of getting wealth this is the most contrary to nature.' At its simplest, the moral objection is that one is getting something for doing nothing. There is no wear and tear on money; in itself it produces nothing; it is a mere barren means of exchange. It was an argument fully endorsed by Aquinas, though it is important to note its wider setting. His view is that 'private property is not opposed to natural law, but is an addition to it, devised by human reason,' a necessary institution in a fallen world, since men work more and dispute less when goods are private. The result is that he sees no wrong in theft, when something is taken for necessary sustenance, and this probably also explains his reluctance to admit that any increase in one's private property could be justified, except what one has achieved by one's personal labour. That is to say, property is seen as a secondary institution for a fallen world, and so in difficult cases — for example, hunger or an attempt to increase one's property — one must fall back on more basic naturalist principles. However that may be, later medieval thinkers, such as Duns Scotus (died 1308) and still more so St Antoninus, Archbishop of Florence (1389–1459), were prepared to argue the lender's case by drawing attention to such factors as the labour and risk involved and the legitimacy of the trader attempting to preserve his present standard of living. But these early attempts to come to terms with the rise of capitalism were not pursued. At the Reformation, on the Protestant side Luther showed no sympathy with what he saw as the corrupting spirit of commerce, and he held up the life of the peasant as the ideal since this was furthest removed from the influence of commerce. Equally Calvin, while more tolerant of trade and accepting the morality of interest, showed no inclination to pursue the ethical issues in any of the detail to be observed in Antoninus' *Summa Theologica Moralis*. But, to be fair, the Counter-Reformation showed no more willingness to come to terms with the modern world; Benedict XIV issued papal condemnations of usury as late as the mid-eighteenth century.

Unfortunately, the history of Christian reflection on what might constitute a just wage is equally depressing. Once again, St Antoninus played a leading role, with his theories being popularized by his contemporary, the Franciscan, St Bernardino of Siena. His reflections were then followed up in the sixteenth and seventeenth centuries by Molina, Lessius and de Lugo. Fogarty in an appendix to his book, *The Just Wage*, usefully summarizes their suggested principles under four headings. First, there is equal pay for equal working capacity, by which is meant that reference should be made to conditions in the labour market as a whole without regard to artificial conditions such as the existence of a local monopoly. Secondly, account must be taken of the common good, of the welfare of the community as a whole, including special obligations to one's family and the poor. Henry of Langenstein, Vice-Chancellor of the University of Paris in the fourteenth century, is in no doubt that this will require a highly controlled economy. Both these principles would be accepted as having continued relevance today. The other two are more contentious, and indicate the inherently conservative nature of their thought, despite their acceptance of a planned economy. Thirdly, there must be avoidance of compensation between conditions. That is to say, rank, prestige and wealth should go together. It was possible to give this condition a charitable interpretation, as de Lugo did, by pointing out that a breakdown in health through bad working conditions is not compensated for by increased wages; the objective should rather be the removal of the bad conditions. But, in general, this principle was interpreted by the fourth, to each according to his status or, as Antoninus put it, 'that the person concerned may be able to manage and provide for himself and others according to his status'. Lessius in fact uses this as a justification for taxation, inasmuch as one can see its imposition as being in order to 'maintain the dignity of the Prince . . . for the labourer is worthy of his hire'. Yet even here one should note that there was also a compassionate side to the principle. For it was in effect a plea for greater stability in wages so that, for instance, a craftsman should never fear sudden poverty nor insufficient resources to buy the tools of his trade. Equally, status was not thought of as just bringing privileges but also social obligations. Langenstein reminds the nobility that their status brings with it the duty of service to the community, and it was a common theme in the popular preaching of St Bernardino. So, it was a responsible conservatism. One might also add that one would be hard put to it to name a single contemporary moral theologian who has devoted an entire book to the ethics of economics in the way Lessius did in his *De Justitia et Jure*. The explanation for the decline in serious reflection here is more difficult to identify, but probably it was due to the conservatism of the theory and the difficulty of adapting it to the more fluid society that was emerging. No one had the imagination or courage to begin again the attempt to apply Catholic principles to the new social situation.

Certainly, papal encyclicals operate at a much less profound level on this issue than was the case with the question of the meaning of work. Still, progress is being made. Leo XIII merely demanded 'that wages ought not to be insufficient to support a frugal and well-behaved wage-earner'. Indeed, when pressed by Cardinal Gossens, Archbishop of

Mechlin, whether this applied only to the worker or also to his family, a reply came from the Vatican that one that supported the worker only might not be contrary to justice, though it would be inconsistent with charity. But, by 1961 John XXIII was taking a much firmer line: 'We consider it our duty to reaffirm that the remuneration of work is not something that can be left to the laws of the market; nor ought it to be fixed arbitrarily . . . which means that workers must be paid a wage which allows them to live a truly human life and to fulfil their family obligations in a worthy manner.' He then goes on to list other factors which 'enter into the assessment of a just wage'. But no attempt is made to suggest how they might be balanced against each other, nor is reference made to the most common sources of complaint, comparative levels of pay as between similar occupations and the maintenance of differentials. Even less is to be found on the question of how just profits might be determined.

So far as the just wage is concerned, one must go back to first principles, which is indeed what John Paul II urges us to do. Wages, he points out, are the 'practical means whereby the vast majority of people can have access to those goods which are intended for common use' and so 'a just wage is the concrete means of verifying the justice of the whole socioeconomic system'. In other words, he is calling us back to the Thomist principle that the division of goods is secondary to the basic naturalist demand that, however society is structured, it must be such that the individual is able to fulfil the potential which God has given him. The right to meaningful work and the right to an adequate wage are thus part and parcel of the same naturalist assumption.

Papal encyclicals do not clearly distinguish between a just wage in the sense of an adequate minimum wage and a fair wage, comparative to other workers. It is to the latter issue that we must now turn. Many Christians these days might be tempted to quote Marx, 'from each according to his ability, to each according to his needs', and argue that this is the strategy most compatible with the demands of love. Certainly, it would be odd if a family failed to abide by this principle. But this does not mean that it is a basic demand of justice, what a person is entitled to as of right, which is how questions of social policy should be determined where an element of compulsion is involved. As we have seen, it is of course true that a person is entitled to expect his society to ensure a minimum wage for him, sufficient to provide the means whereby he is able to realize his self-potential through satisfaction of his basic needs. But there is a vast range of wants and desires beyond this point, the satisfaction of which, though reasonable in itself, cannot be regarded as a prerequisite to the possibility of such self-fulfilment — for example, a large garden or world travel.

That being so, some other principle must be employed. None is likely to be entirely fair. Indeed, it would be danger-ous if a perfectly fair system could be devised, dangerous both economically and theologically: economically because there would not then be sufficient flexibility to ensure job mobility as the economy required it; theologically because there would then be a strong temptation to identify personal worth with material worth. But this is not to say that no improvements can be made. My own view is that, the more inherited advantages are discounted, whether these be genetic (e.g. intelligence) or legal (e.g. wealth), the fairer the system. Greater emphasis can then be placed on reward-ing what depends most on the individual himself, his own efforts and increased responsibility that may accrue to him as a result. Both criteria can be criticized; effort because what may be easy for one man may be exceedingly hard for another, responsibility because power can bring its own compensations. But such difficulties should not be exag-gerated. In practice, rough estimates of an individual's actual efforts as compared with his potential are already being made, for example, in productivity schemes. As for responsibility, provided in the individual's chosen occu-pation there is equality of opportunity to reach the top, it is surely fair to reward the effort expended in terms of training etc. that has led him to secure such a position, as well as the greater efforts that may now be expected of him. If it is objected that effort is also not under a person's control but conditioned early, this seems to me false, and in any case incompatible with the Christian emphasis on personal responsibility, that one is capable of change.

As a matter of fact, even Marxist societies have found it necessary to maintain differentials. In 1963 a Peking journal declared that 'even if pay according to work is bourgeois, it helps socialist reconstruction', while forty years earlier in 1921 Lenin saw his immediate aim in similar terms: 'Not directly relying on enthusiasm, but . . . on the basis of personal interest, personal incentive and business principles, we . . . must set to work'. That this is also what happens in practice is confirmed by Sir Henry Phelps Brown in his book, *The Inequality of Pay*, which is a major comparative study of wage differences in Britain, western and eastern Europe and North America. Particularly interesting to note is that in general he found the same differential ordering of occupations throughout. The only difference was a narrower gap between top and bottom in Soviet economies, though even here there were exceptions; in 1956 in one Russian iron and steel plant the top manager was getting twenty times the wage of the lowest paid manual worker. Some empirical research also suggests that such differentials correspond to what is felt by the workers themselves to be fair. Elliott Jaques for instance, as a result of investigating the views of over 3,000 employees in various industries, came to the conclusion that wages were felt to be fair in so far as they reflected a measurement of the differing 'time span of discretion' involved, i.e. the maximum time lapse over which a person is required to exercise discretion in his job without that discretion being reviewed (labourer up to a day, clerk up to a week, foreman up to a year, general manager up to five years). Though his proposals have been accepted in a number of companies in Britain, the United States and the Netherlands, they have been criticized for failing to take account of other factors such as skill, experience, training and qualifications, though in his defence it could be pointed out that these often accompany increased responsibility.

However, all Phelps Brown thinks such researches, including his own, show is the deep conservatism of human beings. In justification he appeals to the very different attitudes revealed by anthropological research, since apparently primitive hunters and gatherers are egalitarian in approach, with their primary emphasis being on kinship. Marxists too would regard incentives based on differentials as a purely temporary expedient until the false consciousness of competitiveness has been removed. In the light of the Christian emphasis on co-operation, it might be thought that Christianity should adopt a similar view, and simply see differentials as a regrettable, but inevitable, consequence of the Fall. This will not do. For a start, as we noted in the previous chapter, competitiveness is a natural human instinct of which envy is the corruption. Without it there would be no mark against which we could check the extent to which we are fulfilling our innate capacities. Certainly, St Paul had no hesitation in comparing the Christian life itself to such a competition. 'Know ye not that they which run in a race all run, but one receiveth the prize? So run, that ye may obtain' (1 Cor. 9:24). But, in any case, as again the previous chapter demonstrated, given the character of love with its dependence on familiarity, it would be unreasonable psychologically to expect men to co-operate to the same degree in a large, complex industrial society as they ought in a family or a primitive kinship system.

None of this is to say that the present system is perfect. Social adjustments will still be necessary. One such, to which both John XXIII and John Paul II allude, is the state of agricultural workers who, because of the difficulties of effective union organization in scattered communities, often receive remuneration that is not commensurate with their skills, that is to say, when those skills are compared to those of industrial workers. But it is to deny that Christianity is committed to some unrealistic ideal. Interestingly, it is also to suggest that, if 'to each according to his effort' is substituted for 'to each according to his status' to remove the false medieval equation of present social status with divine Providence, then continuity with the previous Catholic tradition is observable, in that the other three conditions in the scheme remain in full force and the legitimacy of differences in wealth is accepted.

So far as profits are concerned, with capitalism there will be four factors to be taken into consideration — the need for reinvestment in new machinery etc., the right of the shareholders to have a return on their risk in investing in the company, the right of the workers to share in the wealth which they have helped to create and the obligation of the company to take account of their social responsibilities, for example, in avoiding pollution. With public ownership of the means of production, these four factors reduce to three with the disappearance of the shareholders, and the last widens since it then becomes legitimate to demand that the public good be taken more widely into account. In assessing the relative merits of the two, what must be avoided at all costs is the confusion of means and ends. For it cannot be claimed that either is inherently Christian or anti-Christian. Rather, Christianity has certain fundamental objectives, and so whether one supports capitalism or socialism must be determined by which of the two, in one's opinion, is most likely to attain these objectives.

One way of expressing these objectives would be to say that the sacredness of each person and the divinely given nature of community must both be preserved. Another would be to say that competitiveness must not be allowed to degenerate into selfishness, the desire to win even through the exploitation of others; nor co-operation degenerate into collectivism, where the whole is seen of such value that individual self-fulfilment is regarded as an irrelevance. Thus expressed, it becomes clear that neither capitalism nor socialism in their pure form can be regarded as legitimate Christian options. Capitalism must be modified by concern for the common good, socialism by the need for personal self-expression. Though the individual is required to make a decision on the likely effectiveness of either system, the Church must stand above both, realizing the deficiencies inherent in both so far as its ultimate objectives are concerned.

It is a point well taken by John Paul II. On the one hand, he attacks what he calls 'rigid capitalism', the view that the right to property is unconditional and not subordinated to the right to common use. On the other hand, he equally attacks socialism in so far as it ignores what he labels 'the personalist argument', the view that provision must be made for a worker 'to be able to know that in his work, even on something that is owned in common, he is working "for himself".' The importance of both elements is also acknowledged in V. A. Demant's *Religion and the Decline of Capitalism*, when he endorses the view of his fellow Christendom Group member, Maurice Reckitt, that 'for the conditions of work to call out the natural associative impulses of men that work must be not only a ministry, something done for the community; it must also be a vocation, done for the good of the work itself'.

But, not only must Catholic moral theology not identify itself with either of the two systems, it must not suppose that the characteristic deficiency of each is never to be found in the other. Certainly, respect for the common good is what is most likely to be violated by capitalism, and individual self-expression by socialism, but instances in the opposite direction are by no means in short supply. Thus, the treatment of the kulaks in Soviet Russia or the Cultural Revolution in China would be violations of the common good on the naturalist account, in that it is no argument that future generations are benefitted if the basic rights of the present generation are violated. Equally, the way much advertizing is conducted in the West can be regarded as an assault on the person's capacity for self-expression. One has only to read Vance Packard's *The Hidden Persuaders* to realize the extent to which advertizing, now a forty-billion-dollar industry in the United States, is reducing our capacity to act by playing on our subconscious motivations. As Packard says, 'all this probing and manipulation . . . has seriously antihumanistic implications'.

INDUSTRIAL DISPUTES

It is undoubtedly here that the Catholic ethical tradition is at its weakest on the ethics of work. For instance, all John Paul has to say on the subject of strikes is that 'while admitting that it is a legitimate means, we must at the same time emphasize that a strike remains, in a sense, an extreme means. It must not be abused; it must not be abused especially for "political" purposes.' In so far as an attempt has been made to work out specific conditions when its use might be justified, the attempt is usually made simply to adapt the conditions applying for a just war. Ronald Preston suggests in *Industrial Conflicts and Their Place in Modern Society* that the following questions should be asked: Is there a just cause? Have all forms of negotiation been exhausted? Will the good achieved outweigh the damage caused? Is there a reasonable chance of success? What harm will be done to innocent parties? Will the strike be carried out by legitimate means? Michael Taylor raises a number of objections against such attempts to apply 'just war' theory. So a start has been made, but current moral theology is still very far from acknowledging the complexity of the issues involved.

One good general point Taylor makes is that procedures based on 'just war' theory, unless handled carefully, can easily exhibit bias against strikers by drawing attention to possible damage caused by the strike while ignoring the wider damage that may already have been caused by, for example, technological change or rationalization schemes. More fundamentally, we need to ask whether it is at all appropriate to see the typical strike in terms of an analogy with war. One suspects that, just as there has often been a failure to appreciate the positive role that competition can play in the ordering of society, so there has been a lack of awareness of the positive value of conflict. Initially, this may seem a rather odd thing for a Christian to say, but one need only recall Jesus' remark that 'I came not to bring peace, but a sword' (Matt. 10:34) and his outburst of anger in the Temple to see that such an attitude is not without

74

dominical authority. My point is not that conflict is sometimes the only way of resolving disputes, though this is true. Rather, it is that conflict is sometimes the only action consistent with human dignity and self-expression, even if no permanent effect is likely to be achieved. Thus, Jesus was powerless to effect a permanent change in Temple procedures, but yet not to have reacted as he did would have been inconsistent with the dignity of his mission as he saw it in relation to his Father's house.

So, similarly with strikes. Quite often, the most appropriate interpretation of them is that they are an expression of the dignity of the worker, with questions of justice only nominally having the dominant role. Thus, Lane and Roberts in their investigation of the Pilkington Glassworks dispute of 1970 found that the seven-week strike in this company with an excellent strike-free history was nonetheless regarded by the workforce as a liberation from paternalism and tremendously increased morale; the workers felt that they had escaped from the image of being merely 'the managed'. Indeed, the dignity of the worker can be so reinforced that as a result productivity increases of its own accord. Thus, Clegg reports that, though the 1912 national coal strike in Britain cost the industry 11 per cent of its annual working time, the loss was only 4 per cent of its expected annual output. There is also the point that, if the worker cannot express himself thus, his dissatisfaction may show itself in a more self-destructive form. At all events, in *Society and Democracy in Germany* Dahrendorf postulates that Germany's good strike record is producing substitute activity in the form of 'the translation of a collective situation into a mass of individual reactions': 'Sinking work morale, growing fluctuation, indeed even sickness and accident rates may be indicators of such redirections of industrial conflict. Some of the workers display an attitude of almost hopeless resentment.' Again, Hyman in his book on *Strikes* endorses Knowles' view that 'figures covering the end period of the Second World War suggest that strikes and absenteeism in coal-mining are to some extent interchangeable' and adds his own comment that

75

the lower labour turnover in the strike-prone car industry, as compared to manufacturing industry generally, may be due to their ready access to such a form of expression for this discontent.

None of this is to deny the relevance of attempting to apply 'just war' principles as, for instance, the extent to which the innocent may be harmed. Rather, it is to note that strikes should not always be interpreted at just their surface level. Sometimes they are best seen as an expression of an underlying general job dissatisfaction, and, if so, it seems preferable that such dissatisfaction should be expressed in this kind of way, a way that is compatible with human dignity, rather than emerge in various forms of psychological malaise. Such an attitude would seem particularly appropriate towards the lightning unofficial strike where technically, according to 'just war' theory, a legitimate authority to authorize the strike is wanting. Such a demand for prior union authorization would, as L. J. MacFarlane puts it, 'require those suffering from an intense and urgent grievance to give way to the decisions of remote officials'. Yet, often, it would surely be better that the expression of resentment were quickly made and thus, hopefully, quickly forgotten.

FURTHER READING

On the right to meaningful work

John XXIII, *Mater et Magistra*, Catholic Truth Society, 1961
John Paul II, *Laborem Exercens*, Catholic Truth Society, 1981
F. Herzberg, *Work and the Nature of Man*, Staples Press, 1968

On justice in wages and profit

J. P. Wogaman, *Christians and the Great Economic Debate*, SCM, 1977
M. Fogarty, *The Just Wage*, Geoffrey Chapman, 1961
R. H. Tawney, *Religion and the Rise of Capitalism*, John Murray, 1926 (currently available in a Penguin edition)

On industrial disputes

R. H. Preston (ed.), *Perspectives on Strikes*, SCM, 1975
R. Hyman, *Strikes*, Fontana/Collins, 1977

4 Choices in Love

With the issues discussed in the previous chapter we noted the necessity for the Catholic tradition to disentangle itself from too literal an identification with specific biblical injunctions and the general biblical frame of reference. For only thus could it apply basic Catholic and biblical principles to the very different social conditions that pertain today. But here, with 'Choices in Love', the situation is quite different. For, as we shall see, the exact reverse is required. At an early stage in its treatment of these issues the Church took a wrong turning, and the fault was compounded by further errors later on. Yet, inherent in the Bible is the necessary means of correction. Fortunately, this is something that is being increasingly acknowledged from within the Catholic tradition itself. First, however, we must be aware of previous wrong turnings so that we can consciously distance ourselves from them. Nowhere is this need more evident than on the question of sexuality itself.

SEXUALITY AND NATURAL LAW

The Bible contains one of the most beautiful celebrations of sexuality ever written, *the Song of Songs*. Although allegorized first in terms of God's love for Israel and then in terms of Christ's love for his Church — the latter was particularly movingly done by St Bernard of Clairvaux in a series of sermons in the twelfth century — there is no doubt that its original intention was simply the celebration of human sexual love, seen both through the eyes of a man (e.g. 4:1—5 and 7:2—7) and through those of a woman (e.g. 5:10—16). Even St Paul, who is often thought to have had a negative view towards sexuality, never claims that his own choice of celibacy is anything more than a personal preference (cf. 1 Cor. 7:25). Moreover, even if, as is commonly supposed, the most lyrical description of married love in the Pauline writings (Eph. 5:25—33) does not come from Paul's own hand, there are passages which are undoubtedly Pauline, where he does not hesitate to describe our physical bodies in their sexual aspect in spiritual terms as 'a shrine of the indwelling Holy Spirit' (1 Cor. 6:19 — NEB).

In fact, it is clear that it is the early Church, particularly St Augustine, who must take the blame for turning the Church in the wholly negative direction which it took. Augustine's contemporary, St Jerome, even on occasion engaged in 'creative' translation, as for instance when he expanded a passage in the book of Tobit (6:16—18). The original certainly recommends prayer prior to first intercourse, but in Jerome's Vulgate translation this is expanded to an exhortation not to 'give oneself to lust as the horse and mule' but instead to spend three days in prayer before the consummation of a marriage. Jerome is by no means an isolated phenomenon. Rather, he typifies the suspicion with which the Church Fathers in general regarded the phenomenon of sex. A little earlier in the fourth century Gregory of Nyssa had described marriage as a 'sad tragedy', a consequence of the Fall; and in this view he was followed by St John Chrysostom. Augustine (354—430) never went that far. The sexual act would, he believed, still have taken place in the Garden of Eden, but it would have been an act entirely of one's free will and directed solely towards reproduction. However, the consequence of the Fall is that the act is now tainted with pleasure that leads us astray and shame is inevitably associated with the act even in marriage. Thus in his great work, *The City of God*, Augustine remarks: 'As to copulation in marriage which, according to the laws of matrimony, must be used for propagation's sake; does it not seek a corner for its performance, though it be honest and lawful? . . . Now what can be the reason for this, unless it be that this lawful act of nature is accompanied with a penalty of shame from our first parents?' Indeed, in one of his sermons he even goes so far as to assume of the Patriarchs that 'if the means could be given them of having children without intercourse with their wives, would they not with joy unspeakable embrace so great a blessing? Would they not with great delight accept it?'

The reason for such negative attitudes is not hard to find. Nor is it one with which the Catholic should be unsympathetic. For above all else the principal motivating factor was a belief that man was called to a life of holiness. Where the Fathers erred was not in their recognition of the arduous nature of obeying such a call, but in seeing the sexual instinct as almost intrinsically opposed to it. As Peter Brown puts it in his biography of St Augustine: 'Of all the appetites, the only one that seemed to Augustine to clash inevitably and permanently with reason, was sexual desire. Augustine knew himself to be potentially a very greedy man: but greed could be controlled; in the High Table atmosphere of Augustine's monastery, it had been possible to "entertain and discuss serious matters" at dinner, but not, Augustine thought, in bed — "for in that business, what man is able to entertain any thought at all, let alone of Wisdom". Thus, at one stroke, Augustine will draw the boundary between the positive and negative elements in human nature along a line dividing the conscious, rational mind from the one "great force", that escaped its control.' Little wonder then that all-out war was regarded as the only really effective solution, with celibacy being seen, even for the married, as a more perfect stage in the pursuit of holiness.

Such attitudes became so firmly entrenched that even Aquinas was unable to reverse them, despite his overall more positive assessment of fallen human nature, as compared to Augustine. Indeed, the tragedy was that through being less vituperative about its alleged Augustinian defects (e.g. though he still places celibacy higher, he treats sexual pleasure as a good) and defending the unconditional goodness of its procreative aspect, he unwittingly made the earlier tradition seem more plausible and so delayed any thorough overhaul until the present century. Although the Church Fathers had appealed to versions of natural law deriving from Stoicism, in confining the sexual act to procreation, they did not do so systematically. Aquinas is in fact the first to set his views in a total, consistently developed, naturalist framework. His position is that man should be seen, as it were, lying at the inmost of three concentric circles. The outermost he shares with all natures and here the rule is that each thing 'tends to conserve its existence according to its own kind'. Next comes what he shares with all animals and here the natural inclination shared, the inbuilt divinely given tendency, is towards the propagation of the species. Finally, there is what is unique to man, 'an inclination to his good as a rational being'. From the outermost circle he then derives an absolute prohibition on suicide, and from the middle the confinement of the sexual act to procreation. His difference from St Augustine lies in his seeing sexual pleasure, when so confined, as a positive good, and indeed he thinks that it would have been more intense, not non-existent, in Paradise.

As an account of the divine intention, Aquinas has an intuitive plausibility which Augustine, with his deep suspicion of sexual pleasure and very low estimate of human nature after the Fall, never had. Herein lay the tragedy for Catholic moral theology — a tragedy whose effects are still being felt today through Paul VI's encyclical of 1968, *Humanae Vitae*, and John Paul II's endorsement of it. But the nature of Aquinas' mistake is not hard to detect. He has simply assumed that the divine purpose must operate in terms of these concentric circles, with what is more general automatically applying to what is more specific. The option he has not considered is that, instead of complete compatibility, the more specific might in fact alter what is most appropriate in terms of the more general. In other words, the good for man as rational being might well affect our understanding of what is good for man as animal.

It was a correction that Thomists increasingly realized was necessary, partly through the impact of the discovery in 1923 that only a fraction of the menstrual cycle is open to fecundation, but more importantly as a result of the influence of the French Catholic philosopher, Gabriel Marcel, who realized that the only way of being loyal to Aquinas' basic naturalist insight that morality is concerned with the fulfilment of the whole man was to jettison his rigid distinction between different aspects of his personhood. The result was that already prior to 1968 many Catholic theologians were advocating a change of position, to take account of the needs of the whole man, as, for instance, the Dutch Dominican, Van Der Marck, whose book, *Love and Fertility*, was published in 1964. Indeed, it is a perspective that even affects the encyclical itself, with one section entitled 'a total vision of man' in which Pope Paul declared that 'it is the whole man and the whole complex of his responsibilities that must be considered'. What is more, with the acceptance of the rhythm method of birth control, the nature of the argument seems to change. It reads more like an appeal to specific Providence: 'To experience the gift of married love while respecting the laws of conception is to acknowledge that one is not the master of the sources of life but rather the minister of the design established by the Creator.' But, just as I indicated in the previous chapter that it is necessary to reject the suggestion that one's present status in life is the will of the Creator, so here we must reject the suggestion that any specific birth of a child is automatically in accordance with his will. Rather, he has given us the power to use our freedom creatively, while at the same time being always available to aid us through his grace in whatever situation we may find ourselves as a result of our own or other's misuse of that freedom.

We have already mentioned that all these difficulties might never have arisen, had closer attention been paid to the biblical witness on the question of sexuality. Ironically, this applies even to the relation between the sexual act and procreation. For, of the two creation accounts, the earlier, written in the tenth century BC (Gen. 2:18–25), fails to make any connection at all, while the other (Gen. 1:26–8), written five hundred years later, sees the connection in terms of a blessing, not an obligation: 'God blessed them, saying to them, "Be fruitful, multiply, fill the earth and conquer it".' Likewise, St Paul does not mention procreation, but sees intercourse in terms of the fulfilment of mutual obligations and the avoidance of fornication (1 Cor. 7.2–5).

In the light of such facts and especially given the current population explosion, it might be thought that Anglicans have little reason to extend sympathy to Roman Catholics in their present predicament. But there are at least three reasons for thinking otherwise. The first is that the Church of England itself changed its position only as recently as the Lambeth Conference of 1930; in 1908 it had given an unconditional condemnation to birth control. Secondly, there was inevitably much less trauma involved in such a change since, unlike Rome, Anglicanism has, wrongly in my view, attached less importance to morals than to doctrine, regarding such questions as less integral to salvation. Finally, despite what one sometimes reads in the press, there is no reason to believe that papal attitudes are a major factor in contributing to the present population crisis. For, not only is 95 per cent of the population of the Third World in countries which have adopted family-planning programmes (Brandt Report), the real motivation for large families lies elsewhere, in the desire to ensure some survivors who will look after one in one's old age or, particularly in Latin America, as an expression of 'machismo' which sees a large family as an indication of one's virility.

Having determined the necessity of widening the context in which sexuality is discussed, the next question is what that context should be. Much secular thinking in fact makes a mistake very analogous to Aquinas' wrong turning on natural law. Like Thomas it treats sexuality as an entirely separate phenomenon. The only difference is that, instead of seeing the fulfilment of the act in procreation, it is now seen in the maximization of the pleasure involved. By contrast to both, an adequate naturalist tradition will try to set sexuality within the context of the fulfilment of the person as a whole, particularly emotionally and psychologically. A person might be very 'good in bed', but neither very content nor emotionally integrated.

It may be objected that what counts as 'fulfilment of personhood', 'integration', 'maturity', etc. will be an entirely arbitrary affair, and so the whole approach is worthless. Certainly, there will be difficulties, but these are often exaggerated. One useful control is the necessity of ensuring that what one says is consonant with the available empirical evidence, what sexologists, psychiatrists and psychologists inform us as a result of their investigations. Of special value are the reflections of those who are competent to speak both on psychiatry and theology. An example in England would be Dr Jack Dominian, author of numerous books on sexual ethics, who is both a Roman Catholic layman and a consultant psychiatrist. An example from the United States would be Donald Goergen, who is both a trained psychiatrist and a Dominican priest. In his book, *The Sexual Celibate*, he has attempted to combine insights from both fields by examining how one distinguishes celibacy from repression. A more controversial illustration of this type of approach, with theologians working at second hand, would be *Human Sexuality: New Directions in Catholic Thought*, edited by Anthony Kosnick. My own view is that Kosnick and his collaborators are at a number of points too simplistic in their approach, but one should note that even they are constrained by the underlying Christian assumption that a capacity to be motivated by love must be a prime determinant of the integrated person's activities.

On such criteria some change in traditional attitudes would seem inevitable. But it is much more difficult to determine their extent, and the debate is likely to continue for some years yet. As an illustration of this we may take the case of masturbation. The inevitability of change is seen in the fact that even the most conservative are unlikely to endorse Aquinas' assessment of the act. For he places it in the class of unnatural acts along with bestiality and homosexuality which he regards as more serious offences than fornication and adultery because they are not open to the possibility of procreation. However, under the impact of the 1948 Kinsey report which showed that 95 per cent of the American male population engages in masturbation at one time or another (a subsequent report showed that it was also true of 70 per cent of the female population), a considerable retreat on the part of moral theologians is to be observed. The question is how far this process should go. Kosnick for example remarks: 'In determining whether masturbation is indicative of emotional immaturity, one must keep in mind that half of college educated adults engage in it.' Even Goergen exhibits a reluctance to describe the practice as sinful for the celibate: 'Masturbation is not completely appropriate for the celibate; neither is it sinful. It is simply a fact of his or her life which he or she accepts insofar as it is there. It is something which one hopes someday to grow beyond.' Such comments indicate an unnecessary degree of evasiveness. For on the Christian view we are all immature in various kinds of ways, and the fact that we are very ready to admit this on issues such as pride or greed — the way in which we try to bolster our esteem with delusions of importance or through acquisition of possessions — should mean that no difficulty is encountered in acknowledging that this applies to lust as well. Thus masturbation would seem to represent either the failure to effect a personal relation or at the very least the temporary treatment of another person as a mere object of fantasy. But from this it by no means follows that it should be treated as a very serious sin. There are many sins that are more deeply rooted and so more difficult to eradicate. Thus the solution is not the elimination of masturbation from the framework of sin, but its demotion to a relatively insignificant place in the total scenario of the growth towards personal maturity and holiness.

One factor that many Christians often regard as highly significant in promoting shallow attitudes to sexuality is the ready availability of pornography, and campaigns are often launched for more rigorous censorship. Certainly, as the most recent official government report in Britain under Professor Bernard Williams recommends, children must be protected and adults have a right not to be confronted by such material on public display. But much more was demanded by many Christians who submitted evidence, and this seems to me to be a mistake for two reasons. First, a choice is more valuable if there are genuine alternatives. God himself endorsed such value when he placed man in the world with free will. Secondly, pornography is but a small item in a much wider phenomenon. Arguably, many a pop record is more alluring towards inducing shallow promiscuity than what the Williams Report call 'the tastelessness and depressing awfulness of pornography', currently read by about four million people monthly. Williams remarks that 'indications from research results are that sexual patterns of behaviour are fixed before reading pornography can exercise any influence'. If so, banning would merely touch the symptoms, not the underlying disease. To deal with the latter would require a radical transformation of society.

MARRIAGE AND CELIBACY

At the end of the previous section I spoke of 'shallow promiscuity' without attempting a justification for the phrase. We must now investigate the reasons why Catholic moral theology is right to place a high premium on an intimate connection between the sexual act and depth of commitment: The bad reasons given in the past have already been noted.

St Paul indicates the heart of the Christian objection. 'Do you not know that your bodies are members of Christ? Shall I therefore take the members of Christ and make them members of a prostitute? Never! Do you not know that he who joins himself to a prostitute becomes one body with her? For as it is written, "The two shall become one flesh" ' (1 Cor. 6:15—16 — RSV). In other words, if

85

with St Paul one regards man as a psychosomatic unity, a unity of body and spirit, then a divorce between those two aspects becomes morally unacceptable. Any deep level of intimacy on the physical plane must necessarily be paralleled on the spiritual plane. To think otherwise would be to return to the artificial division between different aspects of man that characterized medieval naturalism. Modern naturalism, with its emphasis on the whole nature of man, has thus more reason, not less, for refusing to countenance a lack of commitment in sexual relationships. Putting it in more explicitly religious terms, Paul is remarking upon the extreme difficulty of mixed marriages, of claiming an honourable, non-exploitative physical commitment while denying the existence of any attempt to communicate one's deepest self at the psychological level, which for the Christian will mean his identification of himself as part of the body of Christ, the Church.

Within such a framework, the opposition of Christianity not only to promiscuity but also even to trial marriages becomes readily explicable. As J. Dominian puts it:

On the surface this seems an ideal solution. But whatever experience cohabitation gives, it is not the same as marriage. The fact is that its total experience is surrounded by the ultimate knowledge that the couple could split up if they so desired with minimum inconvenience. The freedom alters the whole reality of the experience. (*Marriage, Faith and Love*, p. 193)

Thus, what one finds is in effect dualism, with apparently perfect commitment at the physical level but with an important reserve being maintained at the mental or spiritual level.

Again, however, as with masturbation, we must distinguish between the ideal and what falls short in such a way as to avoid treating sexual sin as the most serious type of sin, which it is not. The Church must show an understanding and awareness of the pressures towards conformity under which people live, though there is of course a distinction to be observed between sympathy and the condoning of an act. Thus it is undoubtedly more difficult to live up to the Christian ideal in contemporary Western society than it is, say, in Communist China where the social climate is still strongly against promiscuity and living together, even prior to marriage. Under such circumstances it would seem appropriate to activate the 'principle of reserve' which we saw Isaac Williams applying to a moral context in chapter 2. That is to say, it is undoubtedly better, if one sees the inevitability of sexual activity, that the individual be encouraged towards relative commitment than no commitment at all. This is not to say that the Church should in any way change its official teaching, but it is to note that a priest or individual Christian may find himself rightly resorting to such interim measures as the only viable means of advancing the individual gradually on the path towards holiness. The danger otherwise is that sexual activity will be treated as the unique exception, as the only case where continually falling short inevitably excludes one from a relation to God. It may be years before, say, an individual brings his temper under control or ceases from envious bitchiness about others. Yet a priest would not dream of discouraging such a person from receiving Communion until it is clear that such offences are unlikely to recur. A similar attitude ought therefore to prevail in respect of imperfect sexual mores.

One should also note that it was only in the eleventh century that marriage in Church became obligatory and that the Catholic view has always been that the presence of a priest is unnecessary for the appropriate type of commitment to have been made. In theory at least, common-law marriage (i.e. living together) might sometimes fully express this. The believer should therefore not automatically look down on such unions. It is just that commitment is more likely to have been honestly and sincerely made, if it is public, whether in a Registry Office or before a priest and two witnesses as the Council of Trent required.

That a major transformation has taken place in the

understanding of what is involved in this commitment, there can be no doubt. This is dramatically illustrated by the contrast between the purposes of marriage as given in the 1662 Book of Common Prayer and in the Church of England's 1980 Alternative Service Book. According to the Prayer Book:

Matrimony was ordained, first, for the procreation of children, to be brought up in the fear and nurture of the Lord . . . Secondly, it was ordained as a remedy against sin, and to avoid fornication; that such persons as have not the gift of continency might marry . . . Thirdly, it was ordained for the mutual society, help and comfort, that the one ought to have of the other, both in prosperity and adversity.

In the 1980 Prayer Book the priorities are exactly reversed, and the middle one is given a positive, rather than a negative, interpretation:

Marriage is given, that husband and wife may comfort and help each other, living faithfully together in need and in plenty, in sorrow and in joy. It is given, that with delight and tenderness they may know each other in love, and, through the joy of their bodily union, may strengthen the union of their hearts and lives. It is given, that they may have children and be blessed in caring for them and bringing them up in accordance with God's will.

The need for this change will probably be appreciated, but it then becomes all the more important to understand what is involved in this commitment 'for better, for worse'. The Bible is very profound on the implications of 'for worse', as we shall shortly see. But 'for better' should not be ignored, as it tells us not only a great deal about the nature of this particular relationship but about the nature of love generally.

However, it is only occasionally that the Bible allows us an insight into the depths of married love, where no

88

adversity is present. Presumably this is partly because its possibility was simply taken as read, and partly because the inequality of the relationship between man and woman assumed in the ancient Near East would often have prevented any real depth of shared experience. Nonetheless, there are biblical examples. We are told that Jacob agreed to serve Laban for seven years so that he could marry his daughter, Rachel: 'And Jacob served seven years for Rachel; and they seemed unto him but a few days, because of the love he had for her' (Gen. 29:20). Again, Elkanah comforts the childless Hannah by asking, 'Am I not more to you than ten sons?' (1 Sam. 1:8). But it is only in the Apocryphal book of Tobit that we have any extended treatment of the mutuality of married love in the absence of any serious suffering, prior to the Christian dispensation. There the relation between Tobias and his bride Sarah is movingly described, particularly in their common prayer together (8:4–9), as is also the more tempestuous but essentially happy relation between his parents, Tobit and Anna.

But it is only in the New Testament that there is an awareness of the possible transforming power of such a relationship. It is St Paul who draws attention to this fact in his remarks on marriages between a Christian and a non-believer. If the heathen partner is willing to stay, divorce is not to take place: 'For the heathen husband now belongs to God through his Christian wife, and the heathen wife through her Christian husband . . . Think of it: as a wife you may be your husband's salvation; as a husband you may be your wife's salvation' (1 Cor. 7:12–16 – NEB). It is a valuable insight that today can be far more widely applied as we realize the extent to which life is a continuous psychological growth that by no means ought to come to an end with the emergence of adulthood. This is why Jack Dominian rightly devotes considerable attention to marriage as a vehicle for growth, though he takes care to warn that this will not be a painless process:

Self-realization within marriage is a mutual process between the spouses and requires patience, effort and sacrifice. The pace and rate of growth will differ for the partners and it will be an expression of love to have the ability to wait for one's partner to advance to the same level as oneself. So much marital breakdown is due to unilateral growth which leaves the other spouse behind and consequently produces alienation between the two. A loving commitment attempts to appreciate in depth the level of development of one's partner and requires a sincere attempt to respond to it. (*Marriage, Faith and Love*, p. 3)

One feature to which he draws particular attention is emotional dependence and the way in which one partner may be only very gradually extricated from a need for constant reassurance which the other partner may find very trying in his or her own newly acquired position of secure self-esteem.

In the Catholic tradition there has been a long history of treating marriage as a sacrament. Various justifications have been offered for this. In the patristic period appeal was made to the root meaning of the word as an 'oath', while subsequently in the medieval period the emphasis moved to the idea of an ontological bond having been established. Nowadays, appeal is most commonly made to Ephesians, chapter 5, and the idea of such love being an effective sign of Christ's love for his Church. This is right. Despite Luther's comment that 'it is nowhere written that he who takes a wife receives the grace of God', every true marriage, secular or otherwise, must be an act of grace, since, insofar as it is a commitment to love, it will be a reflection of the nature of God's activity as God of love. However, while the use of this passage from Ephesians is thus justified, it is unfortunate when theologians only remark on the negative — that is, costly — aspects of the parallel: 'Husbands, love your wives, even as Christ also loved the Church and gave himself for it' (Eph. 5:25). For the passage does refer to the fact of growth, when it continues by saying that Christ gave himself for the Church 'to consecrate it, cleansing it by water and word, so that he

90

might present the Church to himself all glorious, with no stain or wrinkle . . . In the same way men are also bound to love their wives, as they love their own bodies. In loving his wife a man loves himself. For no one ever hated his own body; on the contrary he provides and cares for it' (5:26—9 — NEB). Moreover, the very notion of sacrament suggests the idea of growth. When we are baptized, it is not just this one single act which makes us members of Christ's Body, but rather the sacramental sign marks the beginning of the work of the Holy Spirit who, will we but let him, is transforming us into his Temple. Likewise, with the Eucharist, its effectiveness lies not just in forgiving us our past, but giving us the power to grow in holiness in the future.

But, if the Church needs to take the transforming power of marriage more seriously, this must not be at the expense of its more traditional emphasis on the costly character of love, the kind of love that involves crucifixion in the strength of its commitment to the other. The Dutch Dominican, Edward Schillebeeckx, in his book, *Marriage: Human Reality and Saving Mystery*, has provided us with an impressive analysis of the extent to which God's relation to man is treated in the Bible, on the analogy of a marriage covenant, with God seen as the often deserted but ever-faithful husband. The best-known occurrence of the image is in the prophet Hosea, who compares God's relation to Israel with his own relation with his adulterous wife Gomer (e.g. Hos. 3). But, as Schillebeeckx points out, it is an image also found in Jeremiah (cf. 3:20 and 31:3), Ezekiel (cf. 16:8 and 16:15) and Isaiah (54:5—8). What they all share is the conviction that the divine love cannot be destroyed by infidelity, and thus by implication neither can any human love that is a true reflection of that divine love. This is why, whatever the explanation of the so-called Matthean exception — the fact that Christ in Matthew's Gospel (19:9, 5:32), unlike the others (Mark 10:11 and Luke 16:18), allows adultery as an exception to his absolute prohibition on divorce — it cannot be that Christ regarded it as a legitimate exception. It would make a mockery of the type of love that had already been characterized as the ideal in the Old Testament. Schillebeeckx argues that it must be a later addition of uncertain significance. More conservative scholars have suggested other possibilities, such as that it refers to the Jewish and Roman practice of sometimes legally requiring divorce in such circumstances. Whoever is correct, the important point is what we are told about the nature of love. Not only is it concerned with the growth of the other's personhood, an essentially positive task, it is also willing to expose itself to agonies of hurt in its attempt to remain loyally concerned with that other's good. When, if ever, such concern might legitimately be severed is a question to which we shall turn shortly. But, first, something must be said about that other divine call to love, the call to celibacy.

At present there are one-and-a-half million individuals committed to celibacy in the Roman Catholic Church. Even the Church of England has two thousand in religious orders, compared to eleven thousand diocesan clergy. The issue thus affects no small number of lives, which is one reason why Goergen's book was so warmly welcomed when it came out. It is important, however, to be clear what is meant by celibacy. A single person and a celibate, even when the former leads a chaste life, are by no means synonymous. This is because the type of experiences one is open to will inevitably condition one's entire attitude. In other words, however little one regards each woman or man encountered as a possible life partner, the fact that one envisages this as a live option will inevitably condition the type of behaviour and attitudes that one adopts towards them. Celibacy, like marriage, must thus be seen as a firm commitment, with certain options having been voluntarily closed.

Luther declares in one of his letters that 'whoever attempts to live single presumptuously undertakes the impossible and such temptation of God brings its own reward in uncleanliness of thought and life'. Calvin, though regarding it as a rare gift, is more consistent with the biblical witness in his acknowledgement of it as a legitimate option.

For, though Jeremiah is the only example of someone committed to celibacy in the Old Testament (16:2), Jesus undoubtedly endorsed it as a calling on the same high level as marriage (Matt. 19:12), while Paul places it on an even higher plane, though he emphasizes that it is only his own personal view (1 Cor. 7:6—7). Paul's comments are commonly dismissed as simply the product of his belief in the imminence of the world's end (1 Cor. 7:26, 29). But this is not the entire explanation. For he later goes on to give an unconnected motive: 'The unmarried man cares for the Lord's business; his aim is to please the Lord. But the married man cares for worldly things; his aim is to please his wife' (7:32—3 — NEB). There is a measure of truth in this, though not one which should lead us to say that either state is superior to the other. The legitimate content in Paul's point is that the celibate will have a degree of availability to others that is denied to the married, unless they renege on their commitments to their partner and family. This will be especially so if it is accompanied by a lack of attachment to material possessions and aspirations.

The value of Goergen's book, *The Sexual Celibate*, lies in his insistence that celibacy does not mean the suppression of sexuality but its sublimation, and in the subsequent analysis he offers of what this means. He points out that, though there are differences of emphasis between the different schools of psychiatry, they are all agreed on there being a close connection between sexuality and the gentler emotions such as affection, compassion, etc. Indeed, they are commonly subsumed under the one heading of sexuality and seen as distinct, though related, aspects of the one phenomenon of sexuality, being denoted as respectively its genital aspect and its affective side. How close the connection is, we need not pursue here. Freud, for example, thought that there was a very direct connection and that there would be no tenderness and affection unless genital sexuality is inhibited at some stage of the adolescent's development. One need not go that far, but the fact that our earliest experiences consist of an identification of physical closeness and emotional warmth suggest that there is likely to be some link. At all events, Goergen uses the likelihood of a relation to suggest that, so far from touch or tactility being a danger for the celibate, it is one way in which sublimation occurs when used as an expression of affective, as distinct from genital, sexuality. He is also at pains to point out that celibacy does not preclude the possibility of close relationships. He notes the way in which St John's gospel develops a theology of friendship (see especially 15:12–15), and draws our attention to the large number of close relationships that have existed between celibates in the history of the Church — for example, Jesus and John, Bernard of Clairvaux and William of St Thierry, Francis of Assisi and Clare, and John of the Cross and Teresa of Avila. What needs most emphasis therefore is that celibacy is not something negative, but the sublimation of the genital into the affective that thereby releases the individual into the possibility of a wider service of humanity.

ANNULMENT AND DIVORCE

No matter how close a friendship is, it cannot be as close as the perfect marriage, where every aspect of one's being, physical, mental and spiritual, is shared with the other. But, as we all know, this ideal is seldom fully realized. The question therefore arises whether one should ever say that the point has been reached when it is incapable of further realization.

First, one must be clear about the basis of the Christian hostility to the breaking of the bond. It is closely bound up with the analysis of love we found Newman offering in our second chapter. There we noted that the Christian understanding of love is not universal and impartial but particular and partial, with the ideal conditions for its growth being found in the immediate neighbour. If this is so, the greatest possibilities for depth in love will exist in marriage, with the person whom Dominian calls 'the most precious neighbour'. As Newman says, 'love is a habit, and cannot be attained without actual practice' and it is 'by

94

trying to love our relations and friends, by submitting to their wishes, though contrary to our own, by bearing with their infirmities, by overcoming their occasional wayward-ness by kindness, by dwelling on their excellences, and trying to copy them . . . that we form in our hearts that root of charity'. Nowhere can such advice be put more effectively into practice than in married life, and so the failure of the marriage to survive cannot but call into question whether this kind of love, this particular habitual attitude, was ever in fact present at all. The hostility has thus nothing to do with treating Christ's prohibition of divorce as a law in the sense of an external demand on the individual. Rather, it is because marriage offers the clearest context in which the basic law of love of neighbour, the second great commandment, can be practised, and, just as the latter more general commandment to love can only properly be put into effect if it has been internalized in the habitual dispositions of the individual, so the same applies even more emphatically in the case of marriage.

But things do go wrong, sometimes through no fault of one, or either, of the individuals concerned, and so the question of divorce cannot but arise. Two sorts of justifi-cation are commonly attempted, the more extreme view which refuses to speak of blame, and the more moderate traditional Protestant view which sees matrimonial break-down as a regrettable fact of human sinfulness which nonetheless is entitled to some remedy. The more extreme position is now enshrined in English law. In 1857 the idea of matrimonial offence had been introduced as grounds for divorce. Originally, this had been confined to adultery, but in 1937 this was extended to include desertion, cruelty and incurable insanity. However, as a result of growing pressure for change, partly as a result of the misuse of the law through arranged adulteries etc., a Church of England Commission was set up which produced the report, *Putting Asunder*, in 1966. This facilitated the passing of the Divorce Act of 1969, which substituted for the idea of matrimonial offence the notion of irretrievable breakdown. Evidence for this was taken to include adultery, desertion or unreasonable behaviour, or two years separation by mutual consent, or five years separation when one partner objects to dissolution. The effect can easily be gauged from the statistics. In 1911 there were 650 divorces, in 1961 25,000, in 1971 74,000 and in 1980 148,000. In fact, England now has the highest divorce rate in Western Europe, though the percentage is still lower than in the United States.

Putting Asunder carefully distinguished its own proposal for secular law from any change with regard to the Church's own practice. This is certainly right, for two reasons. First, a church that attempts to impose its views by force rather than by persuasion will inevitably in the end reap a whirlwind. For such imposed views will have no ethical standing at all. The whole Catholic emphasis on the internalization of morals should warn the Church of the dangers of any such shallow approach. This is not to say that the present law is entirely satisfactory. One area where the Church is under a greater obligation to intervene is where the interests of third parties are concerned. Arguably, under the present legislation children are insufficiently protected. At present, there is not enough evidence to assess the full effects, but the fact that in 1980 there were estimated to be 900,000 single-parent families shows the extent of the problem, particularly as most of these parents will either have to work or be dependent on social security. There would seem therefore to be strong grounds for making conditions for divorce more stringent in cases where children are involved. However, one argument for tighter civil law which must be rejected is that the example of others makes it more difficult for those who are honourably trying to maintain their marriages in the face of difficulty to do so. This will not do, because the divorce legislation is only a very small part of a much wider social phenomenon. Indeed, one might plausibly maintain that the Church itself bears a greater share of the blame through its too ready endorsement of the cult of romantic love and its failure to point out the very different nature of Christian love, which will expect major difficulties to be overcome. The other reason for rejecting an equation of secular and

Christian rules is that, although all love is the result of divine grace, there comes a point at which the sort of heroic commitment involved can only reasonably be expected of someone who has an explicit trust in the existence of such divine grace. Locating this point may not be easy, but this is no argument against the fact of its existence.

One unfortunate consequence of the change in secular attitudes is the extent to which this has affected attitudes within the Church. This is reflected in both recent Church of England reports on divorce and remarriage within the Church, the Root Report of 1971 and the Lichfield Report of 1978. Though they advocate qualifications (the former a penitential procedure before remarriage, the latter prior diocesan permission), both are heavily conditioned by secular opinion. Root thinks it relevant to refer to a secular consensus that marriages can die, while Lichfield emphasizes the pastoral opportunities that marriage of the otherwise unchurched can provide. Reflection on remarks like the recent comment of a well-known actress that of all the marriage services she had gone through, she liked her latest, the Anglican, the best, might have given more pause for thought. In other words, it seems to me that there is now no option but to acknowledge the inevitability of a divergence between secular and religious opinion, if one takes seriously the true nature of Christian love.

But, not only must the Church decide its view independently of secular opinion, it must also avoid a cheap kind of compassion. We do not like to admit that we have done wrong, and so there is a natural desire to receive the Church's complete blessing for a marriage a second time round. One can see this motive at work in a pamphlet Monica Furlong has produced for the Mothers' Union on the break-up of her own marriage. Whereas she begins by admitting her own inadequacies, and the pamphlet is impressive in its attempt at self-perception, towards the end there occur these comments:

> What, as a divorced person, makes me intensely angry in official pronouncements, is the suggestion that all

couples who stay together despite their difficulties are performing an heroic Christian act, whereas those who have undergone the ordeal of divorce have somehow let the Christian side down . . . What is rarely suggested is that it may be an act of heroism and integrity to end a marriage that has become destructive, to get up and leave, perhaps at great personal cost. (*Divorce: One Woman's View*, p. 20)

What is worrying in this comment is not its falsehood. It is surely sometimes true. But it could easily be used to justify any marriage break-up since all marital tension has inherent within it both the capacity for destruction and for creation. It seems to me that the Church just cannot avoid bluntly declaring that, as a rule, some fault is present in one or other or both of the partners, that has prevented the potential for destruction, that is present in all human relationships, from being used in this case creatively.

But, it will be said, only here will one be precluded from a second chance, if divorce is not allowed as a possibility. It is this argument that has led many, while admitting the essential sinfulness of divorce, nonetheless to recommend that second marriages be allowed, provided they are accompanied by some penitential recognition of past failures. The argument has recently been put at length from the Evangelical side of the Church of England by David Atkinson in his book, *To Have and to Hold*. He relies heavily on the fact that Jesus refers to the Mosaic legislation allowing divorce as having been 'for the hardness of your hearts' (Matt. 19:8; Mark 10:5) and suggests that Jesus envisaged such an accommodation having to continue because of human sinfulness. But it appears to me unlikely that Christ intended any such permission. The way 'but' is introduced in each passage suggests that an entirely new perspective is being offered. This is particularly clear in Matthew 5, 31–2: 'It has been said . . . But I say unto you'.

On the Catholic side appeal is more commonly made to Orthodox thinking. Here one should remember, as Meyendorff admits in his book, *Marriage: an Orthodox Perspective*, that Orthodox thinking has been heavily conditioned by the fact that it had the duty of remarriage enforced upon it from the time of the Emperor Leo VI (886–912), who even required the Church to bless his fourth marriage. It thus could not have maintained an absolute prohibition, even if it had wanted to. Also, one should remember that it has to apply its teaching either in countries like Greece, where society is less fluid and so the institution of marriage is less under attack than in the West, or in Communist countries where only the devout will desire a religious ceremony. Finally, one should note the severity of the order of service that is employed for remarriage. It is not allowed to take place in the context of the Eucharist, there is a penitential prayer that refers to Rahab the harlot, the contrite publican and the good thief, and the ceremony of the crowning, the heart of the full Orthodox wedding ceremony, is considerably curtailed. By comparison, Atkinson's proposals sound very mild – an opening act of penitence to be said by couple and congregation with the ceremony followed by the Eucharist. But the trouble with both suggestions, as Meyendorff acknowledges, is that 'when a second marriage is obviously a happy event, it is difficult to justify its use and to give an acceptable explanation of it to the couple and congregation'. In other words, the natural happiness of the situation precludes it from being an appropriate point at which to make any judgemental reference to the past. This is why neither Orthodox practice nor Atkinson's proposals ring true. They sound like no more than *ad hoc* solutions to the problem.

My own view is that we cannot now avoid admitting the extent to which secular and Christian understandings of marriage have diverged, and this will mean the Church adjudicating who is properly entitled to a full, 'undoctored' second marriage service. This will necessarily involve trying to discover whether the first marriage was, strictly speaking, a marriage at all, that is to say, whether it was intended by both partners to be a complete and permanent commitment. In addition, the question will also have to be asked whether under present circumstances it can now be meaningfully continued as such, even with the presence of a love that can be characterized as Christian. Such a procedure will no doubt be objected to as juridical, but surely once the Church admits, as it must, that secular courts are not asking the same sort of moral questions as a Christian would, there is no other choice. Otherwise, apart perhaps from a few frills, the Church will simply be regarded — and rightly so — as having endorsed the secular view.

The suggested approach will be in effect to adopt some sort of annulment procedure. In the past such procedures have had a bad press, partly because of the undoubted abuses that existed prior to the Reformation and partly because until recently Roman practice was narrowly legalistic. Considerably more flexibility, however, has been shown, particularly in the United States since 1970, and there is reason to hope that further development along these lines could offer a much more satisfactory solution than mere accommodation to a civil declaration of divorce. It would be unfair to describe this change as due to secular pressure. Rather, it has come from the realization that consent is not simply the mere recitation of vows in Church but the willingness to put these into practice, as the marriage develops. As described by Fr Catoir in his guide, *Catholics and Broken Marriage*, some of the criteria being used sound decidedly vague, e.g. 'lack of maturity' or 'lack of conjugal love'. Presumably how the criteria should be best expressed is still in an experimental stage. Certainly, the specific examples Catoir gives seem plausible. Thus, as an illustration of 'lack of conjugal love', he mentions the case of someone who consistently refuses to provide for his family. Again, for 'lack of maturity' one might think of a girl who enters into a shot-gun marriage at the age of sixteen, only thinking of her immediate dilemma. Another instance of immaturity would be the case of a man who enters into a marriage as an attempt to escape from an admission of his own homosexuality.

Obviously, this is not the place to attempt a complete list of relevant considerations. Careful attention would have to be given not only to the meaning of 'full consent', but also to the impossibility sometimes of the relation continuing, even when full consent was originally present. Apart from the physical death of the partner, there do seem to be several situations that are in effect equivalent to death, so far as the possibility of a continuing relationship is concerned. Remarriage of the other partner is one. Permanent insanity is another, though in this case Christians would naturally feel under an obligation to visit their former partners in mental hospital, if any trace of recognitional capacity remained.

Such guidelines would have to be carefully set for a number of reasons. First, it is important that the Church should have a coherent, defensible theory justifying its actual practice. Then, not only will accusations of arbitrariness be avoided, but also such annulment procedures will be seen as giving a fuller interpretation of Christ's view of marriage, and not as reneging on it. Secondly, one wants to avoid variations in diocesan practice, as has happened in the Episcopal Church in the United States where remarriage of divorcees is allowed on consent of the diocesan bishop with tremendous variations between dioceses as the result. Finally, panel members need to be protected against being carried away by their sympathies of the immediate moment.

This is not to advocate narrowly legalistic procedures. Indeed, much can be said in favour of insisting that the composition of the deciding bodies should be such that they can also function as marriage counsellors. For, if so, Christians could also resort to them for advice, prior to any resort to the secular arm for divorce. That way, many viable marriages might be saved. Certainly, all other alternatives seem depressingly negative. Dominian puts it in a nutshell: 'If a Christian community accepts all marital breakdown, then it has no means of discriminating between marriages which should have survived and those which could not survive because the essential ingredients were never there, nor of encouraging and helping the viable marriages.'

But, if such procedures could be used to identify success-fully 'sinless' breakdowns, where guilt is non-existent or insignificant, there will still be many other cases where individuals wish to proceed to remarriage. What percentage this is likely to be of those connected with the Church is difficult to say. In the United States, there were 30,000 annulments in 1980, compared with an estimated 3 million Roman Catholics who are divorced or in canonically invalid marriages. Some may be deterred by the notion that some remarriages will thereby be declared 'guilty', because it will not be possible for them to be celebrated by the Church. That this is even contemplated as a valid objection shows how far Christians still are from liberating them-selves from an obsession with sexual ethics as the test of moral perfection. In fact, failure occurs in numerous areas and, just as we would not hesitate to admit a notorious gossip or someone suffering from overweening pride to the Eucharist, so there ought to be no hesitation about the welcome accorded to someone whose marriage has failed as a result of their own fault. Nor will it do to appeal to the fact that they are perpetuating a sinful situation; so may be the gossip or the proud person. We all know of such persons whose predicament has lasted for years and years.

In other words, the question of remarriage in Church and admission to the Eucharist must be sharply distinguished. The aid of Christ's presence in the Eucharist must be available to all; for through it even what will remain an objectively wrong situation will sometimes be turned to good. But remarriage in Church is a very different issue. Here one is publicly declaring that no guilt attaches to the new union, that there was in fact no further possibility of Christian love in the former relationship.

HOMOSEXUALITY

In the case of marriage we noted a tendency towards the equation of the ideal with mere realism, and so towards the view that there is nothing inherently wrong with

102

divorce. With homosexuality, however, the most common fault lies in the opposite direction, in the assumption that realism must always mean the ideal, and so anything less than complete abstinence merits unqualified condemnation and, theoretically at least, exclusion from the community. This seems to me quite wrong, and for the same reason that one would not exclude any other failure to live up to the Christian ideal. Just as a second marriage, made possible by an essentially sinful divorce, might, through the aid of Christ expressed in his Body the Church and particularly in his personal presence in the Eucharist, be transformed into a vehicle of his grace, so the same could be said of some homosexual relationships. But, first, attention must be given to the Christian ideal and why it is regarded as such.

In the past attention was invariably directed to various biblical condemnations, and the matter was left there. But, as is being increasingly acknowledged, the matter is far from being that simple. In particular, very few would now claim that the two principal biblical condemnations admit of so straightforward an interpretation. Thus, so far as the destruction of Sodom is concerned, there is an overwhelming consensus among biblical scholars that the original primary grounds of condemnation lay elsewhere. This is suggested, partly by a comparison of Genesis 19 with Judges 19:22f., where a similar story is told and from which it is clear that the primary offence was seen as lying in the outrage involved to the normal rules of hospitality: 'Do nothing so wicked seeing that this man is my guest.' It is a view which is confirmed by the fact that all our earliest references to the destruction of Sodom, if they give a reason, do not mention homosexuality as the cause (Ezek. 16:49–50; Wisdom 10:8; Ecclus. 16:8); likewise in Jesus' allusion, if there is a reference to a cause, it is to the sin of inhospitality: 'When you enter a town and they do not make you welcome . . . I tell you, it will be more bearable for Sodom on the great Day than for that town' (Luke 10:10–12 – NEB). Equally, the other major passage to which appeal is commonly made (Rom. 1:26–27 – NEB)

103

is only concerned with heterosexuals who resort to homosexual practices: 'Their women have exchanged natural intercourse for unnatural, and their men in turn, giving up natural relations with women, burn with lust for one another.'

However, this is certainly not to say that there are no clear condemnations of homosexual practice in the Bible. There undoubtedly are. For example, the association of Sodom with sodomy gained its present currency from some later biblical passages (Jude, v.7; 2 Pet. 2:6—8). Again there are occasional condemnatory references in the Pauline writings (1 Tim. 1:10; 1 Cor. 6:9—11). As for the Old Testament, the Authorized Version gives the impression of more allusions than in fact there are, with its translation, 'sodomite' in passages that the New English Bible now correctly renders as 'male temple prostitute' (e.g. Deut. 23:17); also, such persons may have been expected to have relations with women, not men. That leaves one with the recommendation of the death penalty for such practices in the Levitical Holiness Code (Lev. 20:13; 18:22). Attempts are frequently made to eliminate or reduce the significance of even this limited number of references, either by casting doubt on the precise meaning of the words used, as with Paul, or by suggesting that the main thrust of the objection lies elsewhere, as with the Levitical Code. Thus, in the Church of England Report, *Homosexual Relationships*, the motive is seen as preservation of the family group and of the community as a whole against Canaanite influence, while Scanzoni and Mollenkott, two married American Evangelical women, in their book, *Is the Homosexual My Neighbour?*, emphasize the ritualistic side by drawing a parallel with the prohibition of intercourse during menstruation. But, it is better to call a spade a spade, and acknowledge that there are undoubtedly instances where the Bible offers an unqualified moral condemnation of homosexual acts.

However, it does not follow from this that we must necessarily endorse the biblical attitude. In previous chapters we have already noted two instances where, in my view, the Bible should not be followed, in its prohibition of usury and in its attitude to women. We have no reason to think that God's will for man was always perfectly understood by the biblical authors. While Christian morality must always be based on general biblical principles, one must remember that their application is dependent on empirical facts. Through a misunderstanding of these, specific biblical injunctions may have been produced that we can no longer endorse, because of our different social and psychological knowledge. Nowhere does the Bible indicate any awareness of the fact that a homosexual disposition may not be a matter of free choice, just as nowhere does it entertain the possibility that the inferiority of women may have been socially caused and not have anything to do with their inherent nature. Another factor to take into account is that, if the extensive researches of the historian John Boswell are to be believed, then the present hostility of the Church is only a product of the late Middle Ages, and earlier it had espoused the tolerant attitudes that characterized the classical world. None of this is to suggest that the biblical condemnations are necessarily wrong, but it is to emphasize the importance of investigating whether justifications for them can be found. For, on the naturalist view God's will for man is never arbitrary, and so reasons must be sought over and above any appeal to authority.

That homosexual dispositions in some individuals are ineradicable, is now all but universally accepted. At the same time it is important to remember that there are a much larger number of cases where eradication is possible. The Institute for Sex Research at Indiana University, founded by Kinsey, has devised a scale of zero to six, and various surveys suggest that about a third of all males have homosexual experiences at some point during their lives. Those who are exclusively homosexual are obviously a much smaller proportion. Present estimates suggest that 4–5 per cent remain so throughout their lives, though the figure rises to 8 per cent, if account is taken of those who remain so for a limited period of a few years. The latter figure is of particular importance when considering how to deal with young people who may falsely believe that their present feelings are necessarily permanent.

Earlier, we argued that the sexual act should be seen as an expression of love rather than necessarily directed towards procreation. Given such a view, an increasing body of religious opinion is now coming round to the conviction that such love might be as effectively expressed in a permanent relation between two persons of the same sex. As an Evangelical example of this there is Scanzoni and Mollenkott's book; as a Catholic example one might take a book by the Jesuit, John McNeill, *The Church and the Homosexual*. The trouble with such accounts is that no extended consideration is given to the question of how such a relation might measure up to the Christian ideal. Even the Church of England Report devotes only a few paragraphs to stating, rather incoherently, what it believes to be the ideal. Indeed, only marriage is mentioned, which would automatically preclude the homosexual from ever attaining Christian perfection. But, as we have seen, celibacy is just as much a biblical ideal. What is required is sustained reflection on what it is about these two callings that makes a permanent homosexual relationship necessarily imperfect by comparison. Obviously, we cannot go into the matter in detail here, but attention may be drawn to three types of argument of varying degrees of plausibility.

First, it may be argued that homosexual practice is not in accord with the divine intention in creation. This argument would encounter serious difficulties if it could be shown that the phenomenon was innate, through being produced genetically, but few researchers would now take this view. Even if it did turn out to be so, it could be pointed out that its incidence did not necessarily indicate divine approval, any more than, say, the occurrence of hereditary defects in, for example, Huntington's chorea or sickle-cell anaemia. But the problem is that one would then have to point to some additional feature which indicated its inherent badness rather than it being merely a statistical abnormality like left-handedness. But a similar problem applies, if it

106

is not innate. For one is then required to explain why one should regard homosexuality more seriously than, say, getting overweight, which equally is a misdirection of the body's potential, and clearly also more under the individual's control. Obviously, the answer is that a more fundamental aspect of the divine purpose is being undermined, but one wants this more carefully identified. Since contraception has been defended and homosexuals will always remain a minority, it will not do just to point to the absence of reproduction.

Secondly, assuming a psychological explanation, it could be maintained that homosexuality is a sign of immaturity, best eliminated either by abstinence from homosexual practices or by psychotherapy. Certainly, immaturity is a favoured explanation among psychiatrists. It is, for example, the position adopted by the British psychiatrist, Anthony Storr, in his book *Sexual Deviation*. In fact, until recently it seems to have been the dominant view among Freudians, Adlerians and Jungians alike. But it is now increasingly recognized that it is difficult to generalize, and in 1973 the American Psychiatric Association voted, by a margin of 3 to 2 of those voting, to drop homosexuality from the list of recognized mental disorders. This is not to say that there is no validity left in this argument. Undoubtedly, there are many whose activity simply accentuates their psychological immaturity — for example, a feeling of inferiority towards one's own sex, an irrational fear of the opposite sex, an obsession with youth or a confusion of gentleness with effeminacy. All that need be admitted is that the argument cannot be universalized. However the homosexuality has been caused (one pattern may be the combination of a dominant mother and a weak father), it is clear that it does not always affect psychological maturity. The individual overcomes the original causative factor and becomes a well-balanced, integrated person.

Our third argument, instead of approaching the question negatively, touches on what it is that gives to marriage and celibacy a natural superiority. It is a matter of the nature of Christian love. Even if the homosexual achieves a

107

permanent relationship, this is much more likely to be inward-looking than is the case with either marriage or celibacy. This is because the latter have a naturally creative character that the former lacks.

With marriage it is a matter of the possibility of children and the creative implications this has. For, although each individual sexual act need not have a procreative intention, the marriage as a whole must, if it is to be a truly Christian marriage. Dominian comments: 'It is now increasingly realized that the fundamental unit in the Church is the family, the domestic Church as it has come to be called. It is there, within the relationships of the family, that everyone learns the meaning of love and practises its meaning.' This seems to me to be an extremely important point. For it is not just that children direct the love of the couple outwards; it is also the fact that it is through the family that the possibility of Christian love is conveyed from generation to generation. Obviously, this is true in the trite sense that without children there would be no further generations who could love. But Dominian's point is more profound, for he believes that it is only in the context of the family that the individual learns what is meant by love. This is why he can sum up marital success and problems in terms of a two-act drama.

> For the 90 to 95 per cent of people who marry, life is a two-act drama. Act One is the experience between the child and significant members of its family, and the second act is a repetition and further development of this experience in the marital relationship. The reason for this is that whenever we encounter an intimate affective relationship in life we use ultimately all the emotional experiences learned in the first two decades of life. (*Marriage, Faith and Love*, p. 34)

If it is objected that adopting such an attitude would put childless couples in the same category as the homosexual relationship, my answer would be that they do present a similar danger of inwardness and uncreativity.

Normally this can only be overcome either through the adoption of children or through a strongly motivated move outwards, as, for example, in the deliberately chosen pursuit of some caring occupation. The latter option is theoretically also open to the homosexual couple, and no doubt some succeed through these means in avoiding an introspective inwardness in their relationship. But there is still this difference from the heterosexual couple, that there is no natural tendency for them to seek such an out-let, since a desire for children or a substitute for them is no part of the motivation upon which their relationship is based.

This explains why celibacy too has a natural superiority. For, as we saw earlier, celibacy should not be thought of in negative terms but as a deliberate decision to move out-wards in the ready availability of one's loving service to others. Indeed, there is a sense in which one can also speak meaningfully of the 'offspring' of the celibate, those to whose growth he or she is dedicated. This is easiest to accomplish in the explicitly caring professions such as teaching, medicine and the Church, but there seems no reason why it should be confined as a possibility to them. One could, for example, easily imagine a factory worker having this kind of attitude.

None of these arguments, as I have shown, is entirely without its difficulties. This is equally the case with any other objection that might be brought forward. For example, it is true that homosexual unions are less stable than heterosexual. But there are exceptions where such relationships have lasted a lifetime, and in any case presum-ably part of the explanation for such instability is the lack of social reinforcement. But one should not exaggerate the force of such qualifications attaching to this and every other objection, and thereby allow the exception to make the rule. Rather, in view of the biblical condemnations and the sort of support we have seen for them in the consider-ations adduced, extreme caution would seem necessary. I can see no reason for the Church to change its view in regarding all such conduct as, to varying degrees, inherently sinful, a falling short of the Christian ideal. The wisest course, therefore, is for the homosexual not to contemplate such conduct but attempt the sublimation of his desires. Such a demand is often rejected as unrealistic, but Christianity has never regarded celibacy as an impossible ideal.

But at the same time there will be a need for considerably more realism, understanding and compassion. As already mentioned, as with divorce, God can use an essentially sinful situation creatively, and so one will have to admit the existence of cases where a very high degree of Christian love is being exhibited in such unions. Also, the Principle of Reserve will sometimes need to be applied, where the only effective way of moving an individual from promiscuity will be by encouraging him at least in the short term to a more permanent union. McNeill makes a very effective criticism of traditional attitudes when he remarks: 'If a Catholic homosexual confessed occasional promiscuity, he could receive absolution and be allowed to receive communion in good conscience. If, however, he had entered into a genuine permanent love relationship, he would be judged in "a state of sin", and unless he expressed a willingness to break off that relationship, he would be denied absolution.' In other words, traditional attitudes actually encouraged promiscuity, whereas they should have recognized that sometimes a half-way house is the only realistic option at that particular stage of an individual's development. Above all else what needs to be done is to demote homosexual activity, as indeed all sinful sexual activity, from its status as one of the most heinous of sins.

FURTHER READING

On sexuality and natural law

A. Kosnick (ed.), *Human Sexuality: New Directions in Catholic Thought* (a report for the Catholic Theological Society of America) Search Press, 1977
B. Williams (ed.), *Obscenity and Film Censorship* (a government report). Abridged edition, Cambridge UP, 1981

On marriage and celibacy

E. Schillebeeckx, *Marriage: Human Reality and Saving Mystery*, Sheed and Ward (Stagbooks), 1976

D. Goergen, *The Sexual Celibate*, Seabury Press, New York, 1974

On annulment and divorce

J. Dominian, *Marriage, Faith and Love*, Darton, Longman & Todd, 1981

J. T. Catoir, *Catholics and Broken Marriage*, Ave Maria Press, Notre Dame, Indiana, 1979

On homosexuality

L. Scanzoni and V. R. Mollenkott, *Is the Homosexual My Neighbour?*, SCM, 1978

J. J. McNeill, *The Church and the Homosexual*, Darton, Longman & Todd, 1977

5 Choices in Pain

Many readers will, no doubt, have been dissatisfied by what has been said in previous chapters. Some will have been disturbed by the extent of the change which is taking place in Catholic thinking, while others will feel that it has by no means gone far enough. Both need some kind of answer. To the former group two things may be said. First, what has changed is not the basic theological principles. It was still the Christian understanding of justice as understood in the Thomist view of a right to common use that was being applied in chapter 3. It was still the Christian understanding of love as understood by Newman that was being applied to marriage in chapter 4. What has changed is our understanding of the empirical data, which in turn affects the way in which the theological norms can legitimately be applied. We now see that common use is not just a matter of having enough to eat, but also the fulfilment of various psychological needs, such as self-esteem. Similarly, with marriage, we now realize that full consent is not just a matter of one's signature, but of one's intentions. And so the list might go on. Secondly, in recognizing second-best conduct as a possibility, again no fundamental departure is intended. In the past compassion could be shown in the privacy of private discussion or the confessional. But, with the collapse of private confession and the increasing reluctance of individuals to bare their souls to one another, there is now a need to say more publicly what in the past would only have been said privately. In doing so, however, the Church must continue to be clear about what constitutes the ideal. It should not give the impression of endorsing essentially sinful conduct, even though at the same time it must be at pains to emphasize that in no case does such conduct put the individual beyond the reach of divine forgiveness and that in many cases God can actually turn the essentially sinful situation to the good.

To those whose complaint is that we have not gone far enough, it may be replied that it is not just situation ethicists like Fletcher who are in danger of reducing Christian ethics to a mere aping of the contemporary secular spirit, but Catholic ethicists as well. This comes out particularly clearly in a book like *Absolutes in Moral Theology?*, a collection of articles by Roman Catholic ethicists edited by Charles Curran, perhaps the best known American Catholic writing on the subject today. Much of what is said there is sensible, but the way in which Fromm's rejection of the means—end distinction is endorsed, annulment is contemplated for promiscuous adultery or addiction to alcohol or drugs, or hastening the death process is seen as a possibility, makes one wonder; still more so when, in one of the articles, Milhaven comments that 'contemporary Christian ethicians . . . and Thomas [Aquinas] find in the God of revelation a free Lord who can bypass any moral order among men and any human good and can authorize any means for man to take on his way to God'. He goes on to admit that Aquinas confines such freedom to a few limited cases involving an explicit divine command — for example, Abraham's sacrifice of Isaac (Gen. 22) — but he argues that we should view the dispensation as operating more widely. The exact opposite seems to me to be the case. For now we would wish to say that even those divine commands are no exception. God cannot command what is inherently evil, and so such passages must be interpreted differently. At the very most, Abraham's loyalty was being tested, and certainly he would have been wrong to have done the deed. More generally, what is worrying in much contemporary Catholic writing is the tendency to abandon careful distinctions that have been made in the past in favour of the vague *ad hoc* comments that characterize so much Protestant thought. This is surely a mistake. What is required is greater refinement, not less. That way, not only

113

can past mistakes be avoided, but also possible future errors. An obvious example is the notions of love and consent in marriage, especially if the Church is both to be fair and successfully avoid the official endorsement of sinful situations.

The three issues so far raised all emerge with particular clarity in the theme of the present chapter, 'Choices in Pain'. Thus, on the relevance of empirical data, the Church has already changed its position once on the question of abortion, and may find it necessary to do so again. Even so, the basic theological principle of the unique, non-comparative worth of each individual will remain unassailed. Secondly, suicide is one area that illustrates well the extent to which the Church, while not compromising its ideal, has nonetheless seen the necessity of a more compassionate approach to those who fall short of it. Finally, it is here and in questions of the use of force (chapter 6) that Catholic moral theology has worked out most carefully various distinctions. That these have sometimes resulted in an implausible artificiality or even in callousness, there is no doubt. But the solution is not the abandonment of notions like the 'doctrine of double effect' or the distinction between killing and letting die, but rather their refinement. For only thus will we avoid a worse fate, the gradual sliding away from Christian values into the secular obsession with consequences which we observed in our first chapter.

Pain is an undoubted fact, the presence of which raises moral issues in a number of different ways. However, in this chapter I shall consider only two extreme cases, the questions of abortion and euthanasia. These will not only illustrate the points I have just made; they will also provide an opportunity to direct attention to two central issues, the value attaching to individual human beings and the significance of pain.

ABORTION

A cynic might doubt whether this is a question of pain at all. For, on the one hand, an aborted foetus is aborted painlessly and can feel no pain at the loss of future experiences the prospect of which he is unaware; on the other hand, with abortions currently running at 1.1 million a year in the United States, one might plausibly suggest that the situation has already become like that pertaining for some time in Japan, where there are a similar number of abortions (though for a smaller population) and the practice is simply regarded as an alternative form of contraception without any significant painful dilemmas for the mother. But, irrespective of the attitude of the mother, it is a decision that ought to be regarded as a traumatic one. However, before considering possible justifications for abortion, a more basic question must be raised. For, obviously, the degree of trauma involved is going to be largely determined by whether or not — and, if so, at what stage — one regards the foetus as a person.

The question is certainly an important one. For one's answer may well affect not only how one regards the foetus, but also those who have survived to birth, especially if one chooses as defining personal status a feature that not all post-natal beings share, such as, the ability to form relationships with others, which the newly born and senile are not always able to do. The various alternatives must therefore be examined carefully, both in themselves and for their implications. This can best be done by looking first at the present range of secular opinion and then at competing Christian attitudes. In order to avoid complex terminology we shall simply call that which exists from conception a human being and treat the important question as being the question of when it becomes a person, entitled to be accorded the same value as you or I. (It should however be noted that some of the writers discussed would reject this distinction and treat 'human being' and 'person' as morally equivalent terms, while yet others would see 'human being' as marking the point at which there is definitively present the potential for personhood. The difficulty arises because we sometimes use 'human being' biologically and sometimes morally. Likewise with 'person'; sometimes we use it to refer to existing capacities, those that are characteristically personal, and sometimes we use

115

the term to indicate moral status, that the being in question has a certain worth.)

One suspects that unreflective attitudes commonly adopt either birth or quickening (the time when the mother first feels the foetus kicking in the womb) as the decisive point for personhood. But neither criterion can be sustained. There is no significant difference between the capacities of the human being before and after birth. Likewise with quickening; the mother may well feel differently but we know that the foetus has been alive and interacting with her for a long time previously. It was only while men were ignorant of the biological facts that they were tempted to enshrine this as a test in law. Thus, in the eighteenth century, abortion before quickening was punished less severely in continental law and not at all in England, and it was only in 1837 that the distinction was abolished. Nowadays the laws of both Britain and the United States resort to the criterion of viability, the point at which the foetus is capable of independent existence outside the mother's womb. Thus, the British Abortion Act of 1967 took the period of twenty-eight weeks as the time up to which abortion should be allowed. The period of viability has now been reduced by medical advances to twenty-four weeks and in some cases even to twenty-two, and this is one major reason why changes have been proposed in the British law and why these new times of viability often emerge as a proposed new absolute terminus for abortions. An interesting point is that twenty-four weeks is already the period adopted in the American legislation of 1973. The Supreme Court, in allowing each State to retain or introduce restrictive legislation beyond this point, tried to keep its assumptions in making this decision inaccessible and thus unassailable. Indeed the decision explicitly states that they do not wish to define when life begins: 'We need not resolve the difficult question of when life beings. When those trained in the respective disciplines of medicine, philosophy and theology are unable to arrive at any consensus, the judiciary . . . is not in a position to speculate as to the answer.' But elsewhere in the decision there is the

116

admission that for them the compelling point is viability: 'With respect to the states' important and legitimate interest in potential life, the compelling point is at viability . . . State regulation protective of foetal life after viability has both logical and biological justification.' But, despite being enshrined in the laws of both Britain and the USA, it is hard to see any serious rationale for the concept. Independent existence is such a relative notion. The newly born child certainly won't survive without the help of others for several years. Again, the exact point of viability is being pushed back all the time, with the improvement of incubators etc., and presumably one day the point will be reached at which the entire process can be sustained in an artificial womb. That the advancement of science should determine one's basic moral worth does seem an extraordinary notion.

As the Supreme Court suggested, there is considerable divergence of view among secular philosophers. This can be well illustrated if we take <u>five recent</u> books on the subject − all, with the exception of J. <u>Glover</u>, written by Americans. In *Causing Death and Saving Lives*, Glover adopts a progressive theory of personhood. He writes as follows:

The prospect for drawing a satisfactory line round 'being a person' is poor. There is no single feature whose emergence is in question. We think of people as being conscious, having the ability to form relationships with others, being capable of some degree of thought, having some kind of emotional responses, having some sense of their own identity. But any attempt to pick out one of these features as the person's essential ingredient is implausible. And, if a whole cluster of different factors is involved, there is no special reason to think that they all emerge over the same period or at the same rate. It seems more defensible to abandon the view that there is an abrupt transition to the status of a person and to replace it by the view that being a person is a matter

117

of degree. A one-year-old is much more of a person than a new-born baby or a foetus just before birth, but each of these is more of a person than the embryo. (pp. 127—8)

As might be deduced from this, he regards the killing of the human being as less wrong the fewer such indications are present. As a consequence he is also willing to contemplate infanticide under certain circumstances. A more conservative application of the same type of progressive criterion is to be found in L. W. Sumner's book, *Abortion and Moral Theory*. His view is that sentience, especially the ability to feel pain, is what gives moral value and he points out that this is a matter of degree in the foetus. During the first trimester (the first three months) although 'the fetus will react to unpleasant stimuli by flinching and withdrawing . . . this reaction is probably a reflex and entirely automatic', and so his view is that sentience does not even begin to emerge before sometime during the second trimester. But 'because there is no quantum leap into consciousness during fetal development, there is no clear and sharp boundary between sentient and non-sentient fetuses. There is therefore no precise point at which a fetus acquires moral standing' (p. 150).

A rather different approach is to be found in Philip Devine's book, *The Ethics of Homicide*. His view is that it must be possible to evoke 'at least a modicum of human sympathy' before we would seriously be entitled to consider ourselves as possibly being in the presence of a person. His view is that with the use of photographs of foetuses in the womb 'the latest cut-off point which seems at all defensible on this kind of ground is six weeks'. Obviously he does not regard the criterion as itself sufficient since we also feel sympathy for animals, but he does regard it as the most important factor in determining an appropriate attitude to abortion. Different again are those who adopt a potentiality criterion, who maintain that it is not what one is that matters in assessing personhood but whether the potential is present for characteristically personal activities.

This is the position of both Baruch Brody in *Abortion and the Sanctity of Human Life* and Eiker-Henner Kluge in *The Practice of Death*. Both think that what matters is the actual existence of the specific neural structures that will eventually make possible characteristic personal activity such as thinking. Where they differ is in how much of this neural structure is required. Brody speaks of 'between two and twelve weeks' while Kluge talks of 'several months'.

The reader may well find this range of opinion bewildering, but some kind of response is required from Christian reflection. The progressive one would seem to me to be the one most obviously incompatible with Christian attitudes. For, as we noted in chapter 2, it is not the actual which the Christian values in another, but his potential, the fact that, as St Thomas put it, he is 'capable of eternal happiness'. That is why all human beings are of value irrespective of their actual conduct (e.g. Hitler) or their mental capacity (e.g. the mongoloid child). But, not only is it incompatible with Christian attitudes, it is in conflict with the ordinary unreflective human perspective. To see that this is so, one need only consider the attitude of a mother to her newborn infant and to her ten- or twenty-year old son. Her love will be just as great for the former in virtue of all the unrealized potential she sees in the child, and indeed it may even be greater if the elder son has shown worrying signs of misusing his potential. Equally to be discounted is Devine's suggestion that what matters is the point at which the foetus begins to look like us and so is able to evoke our sympathy. Clearly, as a means of persuading people that there is no essential difference between the human being inside and outside the womb, the use of photographs could be a highly successful propaganda weapon. But it is a two-edged sword. The nearer one gets back to six weeks the more is microscopic enlargement required, and before that there is nothing physical that would engage one's sympathies. But that one should identify a person with a particular physical structure would seem nonsense in any case. The Christian need only recall the persons of the Trinity, but even the non-Christian can be persuaded to adopt the same viewpoint. For he is constantly reminded by science fiction that personality need not depend on looking like a human being. One might be a Martian — whatever they are supposed to look like!

These reflections so far have moved very much in the direction of the potentiality criterion, but this does not necessarily mean adopting precisely the same view as Brody and Kluge. To clarify matters, we may note the range of theological thinking on the issue. Originally the Church adopted the secular view which saw animation, the reception of the soul, as occurring at some point after conception, usually identified as between the thirtieth and fortieth day for the male and between the sixtieth and eightieth for the female. Prior to this point it was held that there was only animal existence and at the earliest stage, the first few days, only vegetative. One finds this position in Augustine, Thomas Aquinas and many others. Abortion before animation was regarded less seriously, though it is important to remember that it was still condemned — partly, of course, because any interference with the sexual process (e.g. contraception) was regarded as wrong. As an illustration, the early seventeenth-century moral theologian, Thomas Sanchez, thought abortion of the unensouled foetus legitimate to conceal adultery, but only provided the woman's life and not just her honour would be in danger, if discovered. Animation and quickening, though originally thought to be distinct, came eventually to be identified in law, as we have seen. All this, however, changed as the reproductive process came to be better understood, with the woman's role no longer being seen as that of a mere receptacle. (The ovum was only discovered in 1827.) The Church's position therefore moved with that of science to seeing conception as the decisive moment, a movement that was aided by the fact that it had already been a minority view in the past (e.g. it was held by Thomas Aquinas' teacher, Albert the Great).

Once again, however, as with philosophy, a range of positions have begun to appear in Christian thought. This is mainly true of Protestantism, but by no means entirely so. At the one extreme there is the position of the American Episcopalian, Joseph Fletcher, who in *Humanhood* has adopted the same sort of progressive understanding as Glover, and like Glover he is also willing to admit the legitimacy of infanticide. A similar view is also adopted by some French Catholics who argue that it is not meaningful to speak of the existence of a person until personal relationships can be established, though they do not advocate infanticide. Such views must be rejected for the same reason as we rejected Glover. Yet other theologians in effect adopt the same criterion as is found in Brody and Kluge, and so we cannot delay any longer raising the question whether this is the right approach. The contention is that it is the brain which makes possible characteristically personal activity, and so one should not regard the potential for personhood as being present until the brain's basic structure is present. Nowadays the point is sometimes added that, since brain death rather than the cessation of breathing is now regarded by doctors as the end of life, so the start of brain activity should be regarded as the beginning of life. One difficulty with this view is which point one should regard as decisive. The basic structure of the cerebral cortex is certainly there by the fortieth day, perhaps earlier, but electrical brain activity is not detectable until the eighth week, and it is only in the twelfth week that one can call the brain structure complete. A more fundamental objection is that it is hard to see why one should not push back the potential to conception, since, though the brain's structure is certainly not present at this point, the genetic coding that will produce that structure undoubtedly is.

But before endorsing the traditional position, one more difficulty stands in the way. This is the phenomenon known as segmentation, which has had a decisive influence on both the Methodist Paul Ramsey and on the Roman Catholic Charles Curran, in leading them to reject conception as the point at which personhood begins. Two arguments are used. First, being a person is closely bound up with being an individual, but up to the fourteenth day

121

what seems to be one entity can suddenly split into twins and occasionally even recombine. Secondly, the rate of spontaneous abortions at this early period is very high, perhaps as high as 50 per cent, and so it is suggested that such aborted human beings cannot possibly be persons since divine providence would not allow the destruction of such a larger percentage of persons who never reach an earthly fulfilment. And, if they are not persons, then neither can the foetal material which survives at that stage be counted as such. But, in answer to the first argument, I fail to see what is wrong with saying that twins simply share a common history prior to segmentation. Their history even after segmentation is after all not going to be that different, given the fact that they continue to share the same womb. As for the prodigality of nature, scientific studies of chromosomes in spontaneous abortions have indicated gross abnormalities in a significant proportion, and it may be that spontaneous abortions are in general nature's way of removing what could not have come to normal birth anyway. I can therefore see no good ground for refusing to identify the beginning of personhood with conception.

I have spent rather long on this question, but, apart from being an important one, the discussion has underlined two facts. First, the Christian if he is to successfully answer secular objections, cannot avoid a concern for detail, and so any attempt to move Catholic moral theology away from such a concern cannot but be a mistake. Secondly, it illustrates the extent to which Christian ethics is dependent on what the facts of the case are (i.e. on empirical detail), and how in consequence its position might change, should conclusive reason be given for viewing these facts differently.

Given this estimate of the value of the foetus, it will come as no surprise that I am opposed to the present British abortion law, responsible for 1¾ million lives between 1967 and 1981. For, while the importance of choice in general precludes intervention where only one person's interest is affected, in the case of abortion more than one person's interest is involved; not only that, but for one of them it is a matter of the most basic right of all, the right of a person to life. By contrast, the 1967 Act allows abortion not only when there is a comparable threat to the mother's life, but also when continuance would involve 'injury to the physical or mental health of the pregnant woman or any existing children of her family greater than if the pregnancy were terminated'. In addition, abortion is allowed if there is 'a substantial risk' of physical or mental abnormalities in the child. Consideration of this last condition will be given in the section on euthanasia.

There is no doubt that abortions are easy to obtain under the physical or mental health criterion. Mental health is an elastic notion, and statistically it can now be argued that there is greater risk to physical health by going to term than by having an abortion, in the sense that there is a greater percentage of resulting deaths, though neither are really statistically significant. But morally the criterion is extremely dubious, because like is not being compared with like, and yet two persons, and so two beings of equal value, are under discussion.

The only really difficult case is where we have in fact like being compared with like, i.e. where the mother's life is also at stake. Traditionally Catholic ethics has dealt with the problem by resort to what is known as the 'doctrine of double effect', and in the light of it has maintained that only sometimes can the decision be made in favour of the mother. It is a doctrine which we shall look at in more detail in the next chapter. Suffice it to say for the moment that it excludes the use of an evil means and insists that, if evil is present, it may only be present as the unwanted result of a good intention. On this basis, a hysterectomy would be allowed in the case of cancer of the womb, the argument being that it is one's intention to save the life of the mother, and it is only an unwanted consequence that the foetus in the womb dies when the womb is removed. A similar argument is used to justify an abortion in the case of an ectopic pregnancy. It is held to be allowable because the good intention is the removal of the fallopian tube containing the foetus in order to save the mother, with it only being an unwanted consequence that the foetus inside dies. By contrast, an abortion involving a craniotomy or changing of the amniotic fluid is held to be immoral. The former case involves a direct crushing of the foetus, an evil means though the end is good. Equally, the amniotic fluid is held to be constitutive of the foetus' existence, and so any attempt to alter this is also held to be a resort to an evil means. However, the whole approach reeks of artificiality. Indeed, one writer has suggested that even a craniotomy can be allowed since what the physician does is not crush the foetus but reduce its dimensions such that as an unwanted consequence the foetus dies. The truth is that in all four cases the foetus' death is just as much unwanted, and too much seems to depend on rather arbitrary descriptions of the acts involved.

But this does not mean that we should resort to a utilitarian comparison of the value of the two lives involved. A much more satisfactory approach is to recognize an analogy with aggression, an approach accepted by both Ramsey and Curran. The point is that in order to defend oneself one is entitled to repel an attack, provided minimum force is used, and this applies, even if one's attacker is not responsible for his actions. Thus, most people do not think that there is any immorality involved in killing a madman or a drunk if that is the only way of warding off an attack on oneself. So likewise with abortion involving a threat to the life of the mother. Like the madman, the foetus presents the threat unwittingly, but nonetheless may legitimately be repelled. Of course, if the day arrives when such repulsion can be achieved without the foetus losing its life, then in accordance with the requirement for minimum force that course must be pursued. There is only one situation not involving a threat to the life of the mother that seems to me might justify an abortion. That is rape. For one can imagine circumstances in which the mother is so distraught that her sanity will seriously be in doubt if the pregnancy is allowed to go to term. If that is a serious possibility, a case can be made for regarding the unfortunate child as itself having unwittingly extended the father's rape, and so itself an unjust aggressor. The ideal would certainly be that the mother should be encouraged to concede to the child its right to life, but because of the total destruction of her personality that might possibly take place during those nine months it is not an ideal which ought to be enshrined in law.

EUTHANASIA

As a result of the invention of the process known as amniocentesis there is now more of an overlap between the ethical problems raised by abortion and those raised by euthanasia. For through tapping the amniotic fluid, usually done at sixteen weeks, it is now possible to detect various abnormalities such as spina bifida and mongolism, and so euthanasia (literally 'a happy death') is inevitably urged as an alternative to what is seen as a life of suffering for the child. The procedure is not without risk — currently there is just over 1 per cent fatality rate — but it is widely practised, especially for those mothers who are known to be at risk, for example women over 45 who have a 4 per cent chance of giving birth to a mongoloid child. In considering the question of euthanasia it might be tempting to simply invoke the sixth commandment, but elsewhere the Bible allows direct killing (e.g. in war) and even seems to allow suicide (e.g. Samson — Judges 16:30). In any case, mere appeals to authority persuade no one. A better approach is to distinguish the three major elements in the question, and to realize that they require separate discussion.

The first of these is when, objectively speaking, one would be better off dead. In much secular thinking this is often treated as though it were a simple matter, but it is certainly not. The need for caution in assessment of the individual's own subjective attitudes is well illustrated by the history of the Church's approach to suicides. Until modern times the person concerned was regarded as a grievous sinner who could not be buried in consecrated ground. Not only that, in England even as late as 1823, people who had committed suicide were still being buried at a crossroads with a stake through their heart, so heinous was their crime taken to be. The reason for such stern opposition need not be discussed here. What is important to note is that it was the increasing realization that the individual's assessment of his situation was completely wrong-headed and often caused by depression that led to a complete change of attitude. In England the law against attempted suicide was repealed in 1961, and Christians would now acknowledge that compassion for such mis-judgement is the more appropriate course; this finds practical expression in the work of the Samaritans, a counselling agency for potential suicides, founded by an Anglican priest, Chad Varah.

But confusions are still widespread, most commonly because of a failure of sympathetic imagination. The person supposes that because he, as present constituted, would not be happy in a particular situation, the person who is in that situation equally cannot be happy. An obvious example is attitudes to the advance of senility. Certainly, if one had one's full mental powers but realized that one was exhibiting externally to others only those of a child, it is unlikely one would be content. But this is not the standard situation in senility. The person is not normally aware of his loss of powers or, if he is, does not regard it as a matter of serious concern. His interests have moved else-where. That some of us will leave this world in something approaching the manner in which we entered it should thus not be a serious cause for concern. It no doubt offends our dignity now, but it will not do so when the onset occurs.

Another illustration would be attitudes to mongolism. From the standpoint of the average adult it may not seem a happy lot, but there is no doubt that the great majority of mongols would regard their situation very differently. Abortion in such cases just cannot be justified as being in the interests of the child. Any such appeal merely cloaks the real motive, which will either be the avoidance of embarrassment or, more honourably, the avoidance of the burdens and strains that will frequently arise for the rest

126

of an existing family. Even with that motive, though, it does not seem to me that abortion is justified. One must still set against such strains a more basic right, the right to life. This objection will also apply to the failure to correct duodenal atresia in a mongoloid child after birth, which is currently a common way of ensuring that the child does not long survive.

As a last example, mention may be made of the work of the Sheffield Clinic, under Dr John Lorber, with spina bifida children. In his pioneering work in the 1960s a policy of indiscriminate aid was pursued, but in the early 1970s he argued for a policy of selectivity that has since been adopted. As we shall see, such selectivity can certainly be justified, where it is a matter of merely prolonging the act of death. What is worrying is the fact that, as David Smith remarks, 'most of those treated patients whom Lorber would now refuse treatment are, in fact, mentally retarded'. Yet, astonishingly, the justification offered was mainly the child's own interest.

Yet, even supposing that 'better off dead' is our considered judgement, it by no means then follows from this that we ought to resort to direct taking of life. When that stage is reached, the second major element in the question comes into play, the distinction between killing and letting die. It is a distinction that is sometimes treated by both secular and religious alike as a mere subterfuge to avoid admitting the occasional legitimacy of direct killing. But much more is involved. What that more is can best be expressed by saying that there is a distinction between cutting off the dying process and a letting go, a death with dignity. There are two main reasons for preferring the latter course. The first, and less important of the two, concerns possible effects on others were a policy of direct euthanasia allowed, an argument that is sometimes known as the wedge argument. It is so called because the contention is that allowance in a small minority of cases would constitute only the thin end of the wedge and soon the practice would spread, once our basic resistance had broken down. It is an argument that is employed in the latest British

Roman Catholic report on the subject, *Euthanasia and Clinical Practice*, where allusion is made to what happened in Nazi Germany and to the refusal of campaign organizations for voluntary euthanasia, such as Exit, to dissociate themselves from the possibility of involuntary euthanasia. It is an argument whose force is often considerably exaggerated. The circumstances which led to the increasing extension of the practice in Germany were highly abnormal, to say the least. But this is not to say that the argument is without any considerable force. Far from it. We have already noted existing indefensible unfavourable assessments of the individual's welfare. One might also note the increasing body of literature which calls into question whether doctors are entitled to our unqualified trust. Two well-known examples would be Ivan Illich's *Limits to Medicine* and the 1980 Reith Lectures, *The Unmasking of Medicine*, by Ian Kennedy.

But for me the decisive argument is the individual's own perspective. There would seem to be all the difference in the world between being hurried off stage, as soon as it is clear that one's hour has come, and a gradual letting go as one patiently awaits death in the presence of family and friends. Admittedly, many deaths these days take place in impersonal hospital wards, but that is not an argument for euthanasia but for improving the situation, which is one of the major objectives behind the hospice movement. Hospices like St Joseph's and St Christopher's in London have managed to give a very different significance to the term 'a good death', as they surround the patient's last moments with loving care.

Much of the reluctance to accept 'letting die' as an adequate solution to the problem in fact stems from misconceptions of what is involved in the notion. For a start, a different degree of responsibility is not the key issue. A decision to 'let die' can in some circumstances be just as morally culpable as killing — for example, the failure to throw a life-buoy to someone who is drowning nearby. So, advocacy of 'letting die' is not intended as a way-out for the doctor of avoiding any responsibility for his patient's death. The form it takes, if not its exact time, will still be largely under his control, and so something for which he is responsible. The horror stories told by Rachels, such as doctors allowing defective children to starve to death, are thus incompatible with a proper application of the 'letting die' principle.

More commonly, however, the misconception lies at the other extreme. It is supposed that 'letting die' must mean the doctor doing absolutely everything to ensure that the patient lives for as long as possible. This is what the principle of the sanctity of life is often taken to mean — the preservation of life at all costs, so intrinsically valuable is it. Horror stories of a different kind are then quoted, such as the protracted deaths of General Franco or President Tito or the 1976 New Jersey case of Karen Quinlan, where the medical authorities, and also initially the law, refused permission to have her taken off a respirator, despite her permanently comatose state. The fact that the Church, in the person of Bishop Joseph Casey, supported Karen's father's request for discontinuation shows that something rather different has traditionally been meant by the principle of 'letting die'. The point is put well in the British Catholic report already mentioned: 'If there is little or no chance of a treatment succeeding in restoring health, modifying handicap, or averting death a patient can rarely be obliged to undergo it. The point may seem obvious. It nonetheless needs labouring since clinicians do sometimes encourage patients to persist in FUTILE treatments'. One way that is sometimes used to express this is the distinction between ordinary and extraordinary means of treatment. It is maintained that one is obliged to accept ordinary means of care but not extraordinary, those involving risk, pain or cost, if there is little prospect of subsequent improvement. As a rough and ready distinction, it has its uses, but one should remember that even ordinary antibiotics will in some contexts become 'extraordinary', for example, when pneumonia, 'the old man's best friend', attacks someone during the terminal phase of another illness.

In short, 'letting die' is anything but a life-at-all-costs approach. It is a matter of a dignified, gradual letting go. Steinbock puts the point well in respect of terminally handicapped children. 'Waiting for them to die may be tough on parents, doctors, and nurses — it isn't necessarily tough on the child. The decision not to operate need not mean a decision to neglect, and it may be possible to make the remaining months of the child's life comfortable, pleasant, and filled with love. If this alternative is possible, surely it is more decent and humane than killing the child' (p. 76).

There would seem no reason why the two elements we have considered so far should not also be acceptable to the non-believer and, if so, then a common mind will have been reached on the vast majority of cases for which euthanasia has been contemplated. However, that will leave a minority of cases involving apparently intractable pain. Most pain can, of course, be reduced to tolerable levels through the use of analgesics, but this is not true for all individuals nor for all forms of pain. An obvious exception is cancer, where about two-thirds of patients with the disease in a far-advanced state experience severe pain. How the pain is perceived is not just a matter of physiology but also of psychology and environment, and a marked increase in tolerance has frequently been observed when patients have been transferred to hospices. But the question must still be raised as to the appropriate ethical attitude to those who fail to respond, as also the more general question of the Christian's attitude to such pain.

My own view would be that a person who commits suicide under such circumstances should be viewed compassionately, but that a very different attitude should be adopted towards the request for some form of institutionalization of euthanasia, with the doctor performing the deed instead of the patient. This is surely the ultimate abnegation of personal responsibility. The individual is capable of taking his own life long before the point is reached at which he is too weak to act, and, even when that stage is reached, he still has the option of refusing all sustenance. This may sound callous, but, apart from seeming to me to be a running away from personal action, there is also the force of the wedge argument to be considered. As for the doctor's attitude in such a case, I can see nothing wrong with him providing sufficient morphine to induce unconsciousness. For his motive will be alleviation of the pain, not the inducement of death, though death will certainly be hastened as an indirect result of his action.

At the beginning of the section we mentioned Samson's suicide. But it should be noted that Christianity has only ever approved what Durkheim called 'altruistic suicide', that is to say, where the intention is to benefit others, not oneself. Captain Oates walking out into the snow on Scott's Antarctic Expedition of 1912, in what turned out to be a fruitless attempt to save the lives of the other members of the expedition, is a good illustration. Why Christianity has never conceded its legitimacy in the case of benefit to oneself is not hard to find. To do so would strike at the very heart of the Christian's attitude to pain. He believes that this is a world created by God in which the existence of pain serves a purpose, for example, by making possible certain virtues such as compassion, sympathy and courage. Not only that, but God the Son personally identified with our pain by dying in agony on the Cross. To refuse pain when it is unavoidable, except through leaving the created world altogether, would therefore to be make the ultimate refusal — the refusal to accept that the created order has a purpose and that God has the ability to give pain a meaning by deepening our courage and faith as we prepare for the light of his presence.

FURTHER READING

On abortion

Bernard Häring, *Medical Ethics*, St Paul Publications, Slough, 1974
Jonathan Glover, *Causing Death and Saving Lives*, Penguin, 1977
    (the clearest example of the opposite extreme to Catholic ethics)

131

On euthanasia

Euthanasia and Clinical Practice (a Roman Catholic report), Linacre Centre, London, 1982

Bonnie Steinbock (ed.), *Killing and Letting Die*, Prentice-Hall, Englewood Cliffs, NJ, 1980

6 Choices in Conflict

So far we have looked at issues very largely in terms of what is required of the individual personally and what he has a right to expect of the state. Only in passing, for example with strikes or my suggestion that the British abortion law should be repealed, have we looked at situations of conflict of interest. To rectify this, we may begin by considering why it is that Catholic ethics has always rejected the view that peaceful means are the only legitimate way of achieving what is good and just.

PACIFISM AND SELF-DEFENCE

At first sight it might seem that the argument against a Christian use of force is an overwhelming one. We need only recall Jesus' own words: 'Ye have heard that it hath been said, An eye for an eye, and a tooth for a tooth: But I say unto you, That ye resist not evil: but whosoever shall smite thee on thy right cheek, turn to him the other also' (Matt. 5:38—9). Again, there are his words to the disciple, identified with Peter in St John's Gospel, who cut off the ear of the high priest's servant in the Garden of Gethsemane: 'Put up again thy sword into its place: for all they that take the sword shall perish by the sword' (Matt. 26:52: John 18:11). Indeed, there is no doubt that the whole thrust of his teaching is pacifist in character, and that apparent occasional endorsements should be seen either as metaphorical (e.g. Matt: 10:34—5; Matt. 11:12) or as ironical (Luke 22:36—8). Moreover, this is undoubtedly the position of the New Testament as a whole. For, apart from the Book of Revelation, images of war are only ever used in a positive sense, spiritually not literally, for example 'Fight the good fight of faith' (1 Tim. 6:12; cf. 2 Tim. 2:3 and Eph. 6:11ff.). Perhaps little wonder then that, as Hornus demonstrates in his book, *It Is Not Lawful For Me to Fight*, the universal witness of the Church during the first three centuries of our era was against it ever being right to use force against another for whatever reason. Tertullian, in *De Idolatria*, declares that 'the Lord, in disarming Peter, ungirded every soldier', and Origen, again writing in the third century, in his *Contra Celsum* is emphatic that 'the Law-giver of the Christian forbade the killing of a human being, teaching that violence done to a man on the part of his own disciples is never right'. Also we know that, though Christians did sometimes serve in the army, they were regarded as second class churchmen and were refused baptism until they left military service.

All this changed with the conversion of the Emperor Constantine, who in 313 issued his Edict of Milan officially tolerating Christianity. Shortly thereafter we find first St Ambrose and then St Augustine defending the legitimacy of war. Hornus sees what happened as 'subservience to worldly ideologies', while Frederick Russell in his book, *The Just War in the Middle Ages*, remarks that through Augustine 'the New Testament doctrines of love and purity of motive were accommodated to the savagery of the Old, and the pacific witness was defeated'. Certainly, it was a stance which effectively died out until the Reformation, which at the one extreme abandoned what constraints had been imposed by the Catholic moral tradition in favour of all-out war and at the other revived the notion of pacifism. Thus, on the one hand, one of the leaders of the Reformation, Zwingli, actually fought and was killed on the field of battle, at Kappel in 1531 (something that had hitherto always been prohibited to the clergy), while Luther, in his tract *Temporal Authority*, even goes so far as to declare that it is 'both Christian and an act of love to kill the enemy without hesitation, to plunder and burn and injure him by every method of warfare until he is conquered'. Yet there was also a revival of pacifism among Anabaptists and Quakers, a particularly well-known example of the latter being the so-called 'Holy Experiment' of William Penn in Pennsylvania in the late seventeenth century. Probably, however, the most influential figure on contemporary Christian pacifism has been the novelist Tolstoy (1828—1910). In essays such as 'Christianity and Pacifism' and 'The Kingdom of God is within you' he expresses the principle of non-violent resistance that has been used so effectively in our own century by Mahatma Gandhi and Martin Luther King.

But, despite the existence of this tradition and its apparent endorsement by Christ, it seems to me that Catholic moral theology was right to pursue a different course, and the time has now come to explain why. There are two separate issues to be borne in mind, first when the threat of force is against some third party and secondly when it is against ourselves. Augustine only really comes to grips with the first of these, and even then not very satisfactorily. His solution is to deny any right to personal self-defence on the grounds that its exercise would be incompatible with Christian love, but at the same time insists that the situation is transformed when one is no longer acting on one's own behalf but on behalf of the state. In the latter case he says one can act without rancour, purely with the motive of securing justice, whether one be a public official or a soldier. It is a solution nowhere systematically pursued, but it is clear that he thinks added credence is given to it by the fact that a reconciliation between the Old Testament and New thus becomes possible. Certainly, it would seem to be the only possible position to adopt for someone who believes that the moral imperatives of the Old Testament have not been superseded by the New, given the degree of bellicosity displayed by the former. In one of the oldest parts of the Old Testament, the Song of Moses (Exod. 15:1—18), we are told that 'the Lord is a man of war'; and numerous moral endorsements are to be found, the classic passage being in Deuteronomy (20:10—18). There two types of warfare are distinguished, depending on whether or not the enemy is within Israel's borders. In the former case the *herem* or sacred ban is to operate under which everything associated with the enemy is to be destroyed (an application can be seen in Joshua 6–7); in the latter only the male population is to be destroyed, with women and children being sold into slavery. It is sometimes claimed that such attitudes disappeared with the prophets, and it is true that a distinction was then made between the enemies of Yahweh and the enemies of Israel, with Yahweh being seen as fighting against an apostate Israel (Jer. 21:5; Isa. 63:10; Isa. 10:5–6), but the final vision is still one in which the heathen nations are brought low with Yahweh fighting on Israel's behalf (Isa. 10:12ff.; Jer. 51).

But, if Augustine's solution is the only possible one for someone who believes in the infallibility of the Bible, our natural attitude is surely to recoil from the savagery of many of its injunctions, and that natural reaction is also theologically justified. For we have already noted at several points in previous chapters the necessity of seeing development in man's understanding of God's moral demands upon him. There has been no stage of history at which the *herem* was morally justified, but it is only gradually that man has come to see this, so easy is it to confuse self-interest or the interest of the nation with God's will. But, if appeal to the Old Testament is therefore closed, the question becomes all the more pressing as to why we should not follow Christ's apparent call to pacifism.

Augustine's position does in fact contain the germ of the solution, even if it has been almost concealed by his too hasty endorsement of the Old Testament. It is a solution that has been well developed by the Methodist Paul Ramsey in *War and the Christian Conscience* and *The Just War*, both of which are in fact heavily influenced by the Catholic moral tradition. He observes that it is one thing to offer one's own cheek when harm is threatened; it is quite another to offer someone else's – to stand by and do nothing to prevent a wrong being done. Love of neighbour would thus seem to compel action. Nor is it difficult to see why Christ makes no reference to this possibility. One needs to remember the specific historical situation in which he spoke, an occupied country in which armed resistance was hopeless but was nonetheless constantly being actively contemplated by extremists such as the Zealots. In such a context he really had no other alternative than to direct the attention of the crowds only to the one-to-one situation. This he does with characteristic brilliance by urging that the arbitrary impositions of the occupying power be accepted without rancour (e.g. Matt. 5:41). It was then left to his Church, which had been promised the guidance of his Spirit (John 16:13), to discover the wider implications of his second great commandment of love, as it applies in very different historical circumstances.

But, if the use of force is sometimes justified as the only way of warding off harm threatened to a neighbour, this still provides no justification for resorting to force in defence of oneself. Augustine thought that there could be no such justification compatible with loving that particular individual, one's assailant. But in this he is surely wrong. There are some circumstances under which one would do him greater harm by not attempting to restrain him, even if this results in some permanent injury. Two examples would be where a prison sentence might be the alternative were he allowed to proceed without hindrance or where it is merely a precipitate action on his part which he would deeply regret after his anger had cooled. But such counter-examples hardly admit of universal application.

What we need to do is to return again to the question of love of neighbour. What is commanded of us is that 'thou shalt love thy neighbour as thyself'. Protestant theologians often argue that this means 'instead of thyself', but for that interpretation there is no justification, and indeed one of the four basic Catholic principles, naturalism, runs directly counter to any such suggestion. Failure to love oneself would in fact be just as much a rejection of God's creation as failure to love others. The failure of so many Protestant ethicists to admit this has had several unfortunate results. Two of these have already been alluded to in previous chapters, a lack of attention to the question of personal development as a moral issue and the confusion of humility with an absence of self-esteem. To these must now be added the failure to see that it may not always be the most Christian thing to do to cede one's rights without any attempt at self-defence. On the contrary, such action can sometimes be not only natural but profoundly Christian.

It was something Aquinas grasped when he rejected Augustine's position, and argued that self-defence is not merely a right but rather a fundamental duty. Admittedly he expresses this, like his views on contraception, in terms that we would find unacceptable today, because of his too simplistic deduction of such duties from the natural order. But he hints at a more satisfactory naturalistic perspective when he writes that 'a man is under a greater obligation to care for his own life than for another's'. As I see it, the point he is making is that simply in virtue of our having been created by God with a certain potential for growth, we have been given a solemn duty to ensure that such growth continues to be possible and that will normally mean warding off harm whenever it is threatened. The objection that Augustine raised, that this must mean abandoning love, can then be answered by saying that, first, there is nothing intrinsically wrong in love of self and, secondly and more importantly, one's aim will not be harm to the other but only the warding off of harm from oneself. Nor is this a mere subterfuge. For, as Aquinas notes, there are tests that indicate where one's true motive lies: 'An act that is properly motivated may, nonetheless, become vitiated if it is not proportionate to the end intended. And this is why someone who uses more violence than is necessary to defend himself will be doing something wrong.' In other words, one must not do more than the minimum necessary to ward off the threatened harm. Anything more will mean yielding to hatred in one's heart. This incidentally was the first explicit appearance of the doctrine of 'double effect'. The argument is that one may only have the good intention of warding off the harm and it is only an unwanted second effect if injury is done to one's assailant, the fact of it being unwanted being tested by whether no more force was used than was necessary to achieve the first good effect.

Some readers may object that this is a complete perversion of Christianity, a turning of Christ's teaching on its head. By no means. Two facts should be borne in mind. The first is that there is no suggestion of retaliation being endorsed. The intention must always be for some good, with deep regret being the only justifiable attitude to whatever injury may be caused as an indirect consequence of one's action. But, secondly, it is not being denied that sometimes the only proper response will be to be, like Christ, 'brought as a lamb to the slaughter' (Isa. 53:7). This will be true whenever attempts at self-defence will only breed further violence. To say that this is always so is clearly nonsense. One need only think of the use of force by the law. As Luther trenchantly puts it: 'If the sword is an unjust thing in fighting, it is also unjust when it punishes evildoers or maintains peace.' And so in this case, unlike marriage, the Sermon on the Mount should not be interpreted universally. Catholic ethics has always believed that Christ spoke sense and that his injunctions are amenable to defence by human reason.

THE 'JUST WAR'

There is no doubt that Aquinas intends his treatment of war to be set in the general context of love. Thus his discussion of the subject occurs under the heading of vices against charity. Peace is treated as one of the effects of charity, and so the various forms of vice against peace are distinguished and discussed: for example, the vice of discord as being against peace in the heart, contentiousness as being against peace on one's lips, and the various forms of offence against peace in deeds — schism, war and sedition. Some of the questions he raised are very much creatures of their time (e.g. whether war may be waged on feast-days). But this does not alter Aquinas' basic insight, that, though war can be an offence against charity, it can also be exactly what charity demands, especially if certain conditions are met, when it will then become a 'just war', a means of securing the basic requirements of charity, justice.

Aquinas proposes three conditions: 'The first is the authority of the sovereign on whose command war is waged . . . Secondly, a just cause is required, namely that those who are attacked are attacked because they deserve it on account of some wrong they have done . . . Thirdly, the right intention of those waging war is required, that is they must intend to promote the good and to avoid evil' (2a, 2ae, 40, 1). In the sixteenth century two Spaniards, Vitoria and Suarez, added a further three conditions, that all other means of rectifying the injustice have failed, that there must be reasonable certainty of the just cause winning and that the manner of conducting the war must be legitimate. It must not be thought, however, that any of these new conditions were completely innovatory. For example, the last had already been extensively discussed among canon lawyers of the twelfth and thirteenth centuries.

More fundamentally, one may question whether these new conditions really add anything new to Aquinas, apart perhaps from clarifying the nature of what has already been demanded. Thus, arguably, they merely indicate various ways in which one might fail to have a right intention, with the allegedly unwanted consequences of the war having become in effect one's real motivation. For example, the demand that there should be a reasonable chance of winning may sound on first hearing as though it were merely a good piece of prudential advice. But there is an important moral aspect involved. For it would seem to provide clear evidence that one's intentions lie elsewhere, if one goes to war knowing that one has no hope of rectifying the injustice. One might pretend to some high-sounding moral objective, incapable of realization, in the hope of being fobbed off with some territory as a consolation prize, when in fact this has been the real motive all along. Again, unless all other means of resolving the problem have been tried first, doubt will remain as to whether one's intention is really to obtain an honourable peace in which the wrong was righted. For the same objective could have been achieved through the use of a lesser degree of force — the threat of its use or indeed no force at all. Finally, even the stipulation about the conduct of the war would seem largely a matter of ensuring the continued presence of a right intention. For armies can very easily be side-tracked into other aims, such as booty.

Similarly, it is arguable that Aquinas' own three conditions are also reducible to the one single important question of right intention. Thus, his first amounts to no more than a definition of what war is, as distinct from a skirmish or revolt. It has either to be a conflict between states that is officially sanctioned or, if within a state, a civil war between the government and opponents who have *de facto* control over certain areas and so constitute a sort of unofficial government. Such information about the meaning of words does not seem important, except perhaps as a reminder to governments that border clashes and suchlike should not be taken as declarations of war. Its inclusion is also unfortunate as suggesting that only conflicts between established governments fall under 'just war' rules, whereas the same considerations apply whether one is dealing with an ordinary war, civil war, insurrection or guerilla activities. Again, all his second condition amounts to is the stipulation that there be something objective in reality corresponding to the wrong which the authority believes itself justified in intending to eradicate. In other words, one might go to war with the right intention, but falsely believing that an injustice has been committed. But we could as well express this by saying that for a war to be just one may only go to war with the sole intention of rectifying what is in reality an injustice.

My aim in reducing these six conditions to one only has been to underline the essential simplicity of the Catholic doctrine of the 'just war'. The sole concern is to ensure that the motive really is a loving one, the eradication of some injustice which has befallen fellow human beings and which can be eliminated in no other way. Of course, it leaves the major question of what constitutes injustice unresolved. But at least by insisting on its identification, it enables an initial assessment to be made and this to be followed up by a constant watch on the conduct of the war to ensure that eradication of the alleged injustice remains the sole aim.

But the doctrine of the 'just war' is concerned not merely with the justice of going to war, *ius ad bellum*, but also with the specific conditions under which it is waged, *ius in bello*. Here attention has concentrated on the exclusion of certain means of securing one's just end, in particular the killing of the innocent. The reason for this ban is not hard to comprehend. It stems from the conviction that only those who have done the original injustice or who perpetuate it by their acts have forfeited the right not to be harmed. Even then, they may only be harmed, if it is the only way of restoring justice. Certainly, there is no suggestion of searching out the guilty so that they may be punished. For, as Aquinas says: 'Considering man in isolation, it is not legitimate to kill any man. Every man, even the sinner, has a nature which God made, and which as such we are bound to love, whereas we violate it by killing him. It nevertheless remains true that sin corrodes the common good and so justifies the killing of the sinner.' In other words, the deed must always be done with regret but sometimes it is the only way of securing the common good, and then it is justified because the guilty have done something to deserve less consideration of their interests. It is the same principle that applies in war as applies in the administration of civil justice. For we would think it wrong to punish an innocent man for a crime he did not commit. But with the guilty we have no such hesitation, especially when we see that imprisoning them is the only way of securing the common good, in this case that of deterring others from committing similar crimes. Indeed, nowadays we would doubt whether corresponding harm should be done — an eye for an eye, a tooth for a tooth — unless such a common good can be demonstrated. This is the major reason why the death penalty has been abolished in so many countries, since the evidence is overwhelming that in itself it has no deterrent value.

But it is often alleged that it is impossible to make any distinctions between innocent and guilty in practice, especially in the conditions of modern warfare where the whole nation's energies are geared towards the war effort, with civilians working in munition factories etc. Many of those in uniform may well be reluctant conscripts, while the real villains of the piece are civilian politicians. But the force of the objection is exaggerated. There would seem no doubt that children are the innocent victims of war, and so there is at least one certain category of the innocent. Again, even with the rest of the population, there will still be a tremendous difference in the statistical likelihood of guilt between the average civilian and the average soldier. Without the latter's active co-operation the war cannot continue. The practice of treating soldiers and civilians differently in war is thus not just a mere convention, though inevitably there will be a certain degree of arbitrariness in particular cases. But this is not to say that civilians may never be treated as guilty. It all depends on the kind of contribution they are making to the war effort. As Michael Walzer puts it:

> The relevant distinction is not between those who work for the war effort and those who do not, but between those who make what soldiers need to fight and those who make what they need to live, like all the rest of us. When it is militarily necessary, workers in a tank factory can be attacked and killed, but not workers in a food processing plant . . . An army, to be sure, has an enormous belly, and it must be fed if it is to fight. But it is not its belly but its arms that make it an army. Those men and women who supply its belly are doing nothing peculiarly warlike. Hence their immunity from attack. (*Just and Unjust Wars*, p. 146)

Paskins and Dockrill in *The Ethics of War* offer the additional point that at least a combatant can normally see a meaning in his death since he is fighting for a purpose, whereas 'the noncombatant cannot find in his own life the meaning of his death'. In other words, where the innocent are threatened in war, death comes as an event to which the individual can attach no significance, and is therefore poignantly tragic.

But, unfortunately, there are circumstances in which military objectives are unattainable without the loss of innocent life. The question therefore arises when, if ever, the pursuit of such objectives is justified under circumstance when such loss is foreseen. It was to answer this question that Vitoria and Suarez further developed the doctrine of 'double effect', the basic structure of which we have already observed in Aquinas' treatment of self-defence. War has this major difference from self-defence that one is on the offensive on behalf of others' rights, and so a direct intention to kill is allowed. But the doctrine still attempts to confine this to combatants, with the death of the innocent only being allowed as an unwanted consequence, like the death of one's assailant in a situation of self-defence.

Nowadays, to ensure that this is so, four conditions are commonly mentioned for the successful application of the doctrine, as a test that there is no evil aim present. First, the act that has the two effects must be morally good or at least morally neutral. So, for instance, an explosion is, technically speaking, a morally neutral act, since it can produce either a good effect (e.g. coal from the ground) or a bad (e.g. the destruction of innocent civilians). Secondly, the direct effect is good and the only intended aim, the indirect effect being merely foreseen, but unwanted. Thirdly, the evil effect is not desired as a means towards some further end. With this third condition it might be objected that in the case of self-defence it is sometimes the case that the death of one's assailant is desired as a means to one's self-protection. But clearly, strictly speaking, it is not his death that is so desired, but his temporary incapacitation. Should he recover, someone acting on double-effect could only be delighted. Finally, the good effect must be sufficiently desirable to compensate for the allowing of the bad effect. The point here is that a stage will be reached at which the bad effect is so out of proportion to the good effect that it becomes implausible to continue to claim that the bad effect is not part of one's aim.

All this probably sounds unnecessarily technical. The aim, however, is a good one, of trying to clarify when it becomes a mere pretence to claim that the bad effect of one's action is only an unwanted consequence and no part of one's design. An illustration would be if the death of civilians is essential as a means to some further purposes one has. For example, one might wish to instill fear into the enemy population, in which case, unlike the self-defence situation referred to above, there would be no joy if the casualties turned out to have been incapacitated for only a few minutes. Again, if there is considerable loss of civilian life as the result of the bombing of what is, from the military point of view, a relatively insignificant target the fourth condition, the principle of proportionality, will have been violated. These cases can then be contrasted with the situation in which there is, say, a key military installation near a town, where the military do everything possible to keep civilian casualties to a minimum but nonetheless see the inevitability of some occurring.

It was the doctrine of 'double effect' which George Bell, Bishop of Chichester, was applying when he protested against British area-bombing of German cities during the last war. For the loss of civilian life was so out of proportion to the strategic importance of the alleged military targets that the only possible inference that could be drawn was that the real intention lay elsewhere. The Prime Minister, Winston Churchill, never publicly admitted this and in his speeches endorsed 'just war' theory, but we now know that the aim of Sir Arthur Harris, Commander-in-Chief, Bomber Command, was the collapse of civilian morale. As he put it, 'in Bomber Command we have always worked on the principle that bombing anything in Germany is better than bombing nothing'.

NUCLEAR WAR

The Second World War is probably the clearest case on record of a war whose cause was just. But, as we have noted, it cannot be claimed that it was consistently waged justly. The British bombing assault upon Dresden in particular can only be described as utterly immoral. Such conflict between theory and practice might be taken as proof of the unfeasibility of applying 'just war' theory. But this would be wrong. Compassion for those suffering in occupied Europe, combined with the realization that those bearing arms for such an evil regime had forfeited their right to life for so long as they continued to do so, is sufficient justification. What rather is indicated is the need for more churchmen of the stature of Bishop Bell to put moral pressure on their governments, as soon as they see violations.

Another such violation occurred at the very end of the war in the bombing of Hiroshima and Nagasaki. In chapter 1 we noted the way in which Fletcher referred to the decision having been made on 'a vast scale of agapeistic calculus', and it is certainly true that the United States Army estimated that a million Allied casualties might otherwise have been involved, though the Navy's estimate was considerably less. But even if we assume this figure and set it against the 105,000 killed and 115,000 injured, it would still not have justified the dropping of the two bombs on 'just war' theory. This may seem madness, but the point is that there can be no moral trade-off against purely innocent lives, who have done nothing to deserve forfeiting their rights. For, although there were some minor military targets, the scale of civilian casualties leaves no doubt that the real motive was to wreak such loss of life that the Japanese would be cowered into surrender. If it is objected that the Allied troops would be just as innocent, one need only recall the women and children involved to see the falsity of this, and in any case in bearing arms in a just war one is trying to secure justice for others, even if this means the loss of one's own life. The irony is that the real American motive seems to have been determination that the Soviet Union should not share in the spoils.

But, if the only actual use of nuclear weapons to date was not justified, the question must still be faced as to whether their use could ever be. It is sometimes argued that such a war could be waged, if only military targets were aimed at, rather than cities. Paul Ramsey is one person who takes such a view. United States policy, after Robert McNamara became Defence Secretary in 1960, was based on the theory of mutually assured destruction, popularly abbreviated to MAD. According to this theory, the USSR was deterred by missiles so aimed that, if it attacked, retaliation would be on a massive scale, with the 200 largest cities of the USSR being hit (together these constitute about a third of the country's population). However, this policy was changed in 1979 with President Carter's Presidential Directive 59 by which retaliation was ordered against military targets. The reasons were partly moral and partly the feeling that more options would be left open this way. Sir Solly Zuckerman comments that 'in view of the enormous size of the nuclear armouries of the USA and the USSR, one dare not lose sight of the fact that from the operational point of view there is practically no difference'. He makes two important points. The first is that, since military headquarters are normally in capital cities (e.g the Pentagon in Washington, the Ministry of Defence in London), cities are still going to be direct targets. Secondly, although the accuracy of nuclear weapons has improved enormously, when the CEP (circular error probable) is given as, say, 400 yards,

> . . . what is meant is that both calculation and such tests as have been made indicate that fifty per cent of shots fired at a given target will fall within a circle of that particular radius whose centre is the aiming point . . . but such estimates of accuracy presuppose that every step in the process from launch to strike works according to plan . . . [and] above all, what the calculation of CEPs does not mean is that the fifty

per cent of the shots which it is estimated will fall outside a given radius will necessarily have a normal distribution. (*Nuclear Illusion and Reality*, p. 24)

In other words, CEPs assume ideal conditions and in the 50 per cent of cases that go outside the limit there is no guarantee that they will go only narrowly away from the target rather than, say, five miles. But, not only has it been argued that there is no difference practically, it has also been claimed that there is no difference morally. This is the view taken in the collection of essays, *Nuclear Weapons: A Catholic Response*. Kenny, in his contribution, readily concedes that there could be a considerable difference in the number of casualties involved as between a counter-force strategy, one aimed at military targets, and a counter-value strategy, one in which there were civilian targets. He quotes figures which suggest that in the latter case the loss of life in Western Europe and the United States would amount to 215 million dead, whereas on the former approach this would be reduced to 25 million. However, he then goes on to remark: 'To claim that a counterforce strategy of this kind does not involve an attack on civilian populations is like claiming not to be responsible for the death of a friend if one shoots a bullet to kill a mosquito perched on his throat.'

The point of this graphic analogy is not the certainty of the consequence but its lack of proportion to what is being aimed at. Thus, just as the death of one's friend is out of proportion to the killing of the mosquito, so the civilian casualties are out of all proportion to whatever good is being aimed at. That being so, the fourth condition for the correct application of the doctrine of 'double effect' — the principle of proportionality — is being violated and so, contrary to what is claimed, one must see the death of the civilians as part of one's plan, one's direct intention. That is why Kenny ends his article with the comment: 'The prospect of standing defenceless before Communist Russia is indeed a sombre one. But that does not justify us in covenanting with the NATO powers to commit murder.'

148

However, it is not an argument that automatically scotches all forms of limited nuclear war. For example, one might try to recover proportionality by increasing the good effect and decreasing the bad. The former could be done by imagining an enemy bent on mass extermination of peoples rather than just the limitations of freedom that would arise under Soviet rule. But that is not the situation with which we are faced. So the more common strategy is to suggest that casualties need not be as horrendous as Kenny suggests. General Sir John Hackett, for example, in his book, *The Third World War, August 1985*, provides us with a scenario which ends happily for the West, though Birmingham and Minsk are eliminated in the brief exchange.

Indeed, the whole tenor of current Western military thought seems based on the assumption that escalation can be avoided, and a limited war take place. This expresses itself in the doctrine known as 'flexible response', according to which, in the words of former US Defence Secretary, Harold Brown, 'any Soviet planner must consider that a successful Soviet massive conventional attack would trigger first tactical, then strategic nuclear weapons used against them'. NATO has in fact never renounced its right to be the first to use nuclear weapons, so worried is it by the alleged superiority of the Soviet Union in conventional forces. But the very notion of such a limited war is nonsense for two reasons. First, in such a crisis there will inevitably be the temptation to try the next stage up if one is losing, or even perhaps if one is winning, especially as a pre-emptive strike might be successful in preventing one's opponent from himself escalating to the next stage. The situation is thus inherently unstable. But, secondly, and more importantly, all we know of Soviet intentions suggests that they will automatically assume that it is all-out war. Such at any rate is the view of Marshal Sokolovskii, author of *Military Strategy*, the most commonly quoted source for Soviet attitudes on the subject. Nor is this position difficult to comprehend. For in the Second World War they experienced just such an all-out war, with 20 million dead and two-thirds of their industrial base destroyed.

With that experience behind them they do not expect any gentlemanly conventions to be obeyed and so, if nuclear weapons are used by the West, it will be natural for them to assume that this means all-out war.

Thus, our conclusion is that, while in theory it might be possible to envisage a use of nuclear weapons that is consonant with 'just war' theory, in practice this is not so. But, even supposing their use is not justified, it might be the case that an argument can be found for threatening their use. Certainly, it is a very odd notion of deterrent in use when Britain is claimed to have a deterrent and yet the United States has a nuclear arsenal that is fifty to a hundred times larger. In mentioning this fact I do not wish to call into question whether Britain is in fact in possession of a deterrent, but to point out that what matters in a threat is not the absolute amount of damage done, but whether the damage is sufficient to worry the enemy. But, if that is so, the Soviet Union must be as worried about the possibility of Britain being able to destroy one of its major cities like Leningrad or Moscow as it is by the United States being able to destroy its entire territory several times over. Reluctance to go to war does not keep on increasing proportionally, the more damage is threatened. As soon as something of major value is threatened, that is the decisive cut-off point, after which any additional threat will only have marginal impact.

That being so, the arms race can only be viewed as an absurdity. It was President Carter who noted the fact that a single Poseidon submarine has the capacity to destroy every major city in the USSR. Now, of course, to be an effective threat one has to be sure of some of one's weapons reaching their target, but no one doubts this would be so in the great majority of cases. Part of the problem is simply national pride about being in the lead. Someone at this point might mention Cuba, but, even if the United States had been the inferior power, it is doubtful whether Krushchev would have risked enormous destruction in the Soviet Union for so small a prize. Another dimension of the problem is competitiveness between the different branches of the armed forces. Each of them, air, land and sea, wishes to be fully effective on its own. This is the cause of the current debate about Cruise missiles. With planes in the air and nuclear submarines, there already are plenty of missiles on the move that are therefore extremely difficult to hit, even with the improvement in CEP that has taken place. Yet it is insisted that Cruise missiles capable of being launched from mobile land-based vehicles be introduced into Europe to replace the stationary missile silos, thereby vastly increasing the territory that has to be destroyed if they are to be eliminated by an enemy.

At present there are at least 50,000 nuclear warheads in existence with a total explosive capacity of a million times greater than the first atomic bomb that was dropped on Hiroshima. It is little wonder then that there has been a revival of interest in the Campaign for Nuclear Disarmament, with several recent books putting forward the case (e.g. *Protest and Survive*, edited by E. P. Thompson and Dan Smith, or *As Lambs to the Slaughter* by members of the Bradford School of Peace Studies). We have already admitted that in theory, though not in practice, a 'just war' could be fought with nuclear weapons. It might therefore be thought that there will be no difficulty in endorsing their role as a deterrent. But the problem is in fact greater. For, as we have observed, deterrents are at their most effective when something valuable is threatened, and that will mean cities — directly threatening to kill the innocent. The intention is thus worse, not better, than in the theoretically justified nuclear war. Some Protestant theologians try to get round the problem by redescription. Thielicke talks about a 'balance of unreadiness' to use the weapons, Ramsey about the threat of something disproportionate not necessarily being a disproportionate threat. But there would seem to me to be no alternative but to acknowledge the immorality of the threat and so endeavour to extricate oneself from it as soon as possible. I can see only advantages for Britain in unilateral disarmament, provided, that is, that our conventional means of defence are maintained and strengthened. In the case of the United

151

States, given its superiority in arms, there is a special obligation to see that other nuclear powers follow suit. But, with a greater willingness to make concessions at the SALT talks, this does not seem beyond the bounds of possibility. After all, the United States is four to seven years technologically ahead of the Soviet Union and, as J. A. Joyce remarks in *The War Machine*, 'studies of the Soviet economy reveal that Moscow has been able to meet each new threat from the Pentagon only by heavy economic and social sacrifices'.

CONFLICT WITHIN THE STATE

Partly because of biblical comments like those of Paul that 'the powers that be are ordained of God' (Rom. 13:1) and partly because of the tendency noted elsewhere of identifying divine Providence with the way the world at present is, there has always been within the Catholic tradition strong resistance to the use of force against the state. Dante, for example, banished the murderers of Caesar to the depths of the Inferno, and the Council of Constance (1414—18) prohibited tyrannicide. But it is an attitude that is rightly changing. We are now more fully aware of our responsibility for the way the world is, and that, regrettably, force is sometimes the only way of effecting change. There are occasional early anticipations of this attitude. The most famous is perhaps that of John of Salisbury, writing in the twelfth century. Referring to stories like those of Jael and Sisera (Judges 4:18ff.) and Judith and Holophernes (in the Apocryphal book of Judith), he argues that there is a basic difference between a good king who, in observing the law, was a guardian of the well-being of his people and the oppressor whose rule was merely based on force. His conclusion is that, like Sisera and Holophernes, he who usurps the sword deserves to die by the sword.

Fortunately, in a democracy things need not go that far. From the Christian point of view it is the form of government that is most readily defensible. For it is most naturally suited to allowing the full development of the individual's potential, particularly his potential for self-expression. But, even so, this is not always what happens. Majorities can be heartless in their neglect of minority interests. We should not forget that Hitler came to power legally in a democracy, and not as a result of revolution. That being so, even in a democracy there may be circumstances in which the ballot box fails to prove an adequate solution. This is not an argument for an immediate resort to violence. But its use might be justified as a last resort in a situation of extreme threat to others. Thus, suppose Germany had remained a democracy under Hitler. The German theologian, Dietrich Bonhoeffer, would still have been justified in joining the resistance movement that culminated in the unsuccessful attempt on Hitler's life in July 1944.

But, as an almost inviolable rule, lesser measures in defence of minorities will suffice. It is here that the Church can play a particularly useful role, acting as the nation's conscience, as it were. In present-day Britain this would mean drawing attention to such varied facts as: the disadvantages the black community labours under in the ghettoes that have developed in British cities, such as Toxteth in Liverpool and Brixton in London; the morally debilitating effects of long-term unemployment; the exploitation of nurses and farmworkers that results from their inability to organize effective strike action, etc. The Church thus cannot avoid being 'political' to some degree. But, if its voice is to be heeded, there must be no hint of party political bias. That is why clergy publicly endorsing a particular political party are really acting against the best interests of the most disadvantaged in our society. For they enable critics to claim that the Church is doing no more than reflecting the political bias of its members. If national churches and individual Christians took as much care as is shown in twentieth-century paper encyclicals, then men would have no choice but to acknowledge that it is a moral judgement alone that is being made.

But it is not just words that will be required of the Church but also action. Sometimes all that will be possible is that devoted priests should live and work among the

153

disadvantaged. Little as it may appear, such identification is often valued out of all proportion to its apparent significance. This is because in these days of easy mobility the Church is frequently the only caring profession that continues to reside in the depressed community. At other times, it will mean far more dramatic action involving passive resistance to the will of the majority, as in Martin Luther King's campaign in the 1960s for basic human rights for blacks in the United States.

But, whether in word or action, the Christian in a democracy has a very easy task compared to the dilemma confronting many of our fellow Christians in non-democratic societies. This is not to say that all such governments ought automatically to be opposed. Far from it. In the first place, although democracy must be the ideal, in some countries the only realistic option is some form of single-party state. An obvious case is that of many newly independent African states where the traditional party system would merely exacerbate tribal divisions and so prevent the binding power that comes through the formation of a national consciousness. But, secondly, not only does force remain a policy of last resort, its use in many cases would be counter-productive. A striking example of the latter is what happened with the Tupamaros guerrillas in Uruguay. Their aim had been the improvement of the lot of the disadvantaged in an already existing democracy. The result was a backlash with the overthrow of that democracy by a right-wing dictatorship, resulting in even worse conditions for the poor. Indeed, the difficulty of calculating the likely effects of violence within a state is so much more acute than in normal warfare, that it is not really surprising to find Christians advocating restraint even in the face of brutal dictatorships. Writing in 1968 when Brazil was still under just such a regime, that of General Castello Branco, with torture and oppression rife, Helder Camara, Archbishop of Recife, did not hesitate to declare that 'personally, I would prefer a thousand times to be killed than to kill'. The interesting thing is that, in this case at least, passive but outspoken opposition has in fact paid off. For thanks in large part to his courageous stand and that of other churchmen in the country (e.g. Cardinal Arns), Brazil under President Figueiredo had become, by mid-1980, a country without political prisoners and without torture.

But in the same paragraph of *Church and Colonialism* where Camara makes that comment, he also acknowledges the argument on the other side: 'I respect those who feel obliged in conscience to opt for violence ... In my opinion, the memory of Camilo Torres and of Che Guevara merits as much respect as that of Martin Luther King. I accuse the real authors of violence.' Camilo Torres was a priest who was eventually killed fighting as a guerrilla in Colombia in 1966. Nor is he by any means an isolated example of Christians who have joined such movements. Another example would be Ernesto Cardenal's involvement with the Sandanista guerrilla movement, which successfully overthrew the long-standing dictatorship of the Somoza family in Nicaragua in 1979. That being so, it will be useful to end our discussion of choices in conflict by looking briefly at the morality of terrorism and the most common government response, the use of torture.

The first thing that must be guarded against is the manipulation of our sympathies by the use of words. Thus, there is not much difference between the type of conduct that is being referred to when one talks of guerrilla, freedom fighter or terrorist. But there is a tremendous difference in attitudes implied. 'Guerrilla' is a fairly neutral term, whereas 'freedom fighter' indicates endorsement of the cause being fought for and 'terrorist' implies hostile antipathy. Yet all the word 'terrorist' does is indicate more clearly the type of tactics that have to be employed in such situations. As an ancient Chinese proverb puts it, 'Kill one, frighten ten thousand'. In other words, the aim is so to demoralize the government and its enforcement agencies that it is compelled to concede defeat. That the installation of fear could be a moral act in war, I have no doubt. Indeed, in ordinary warfare, it is often the kinder course, as when the enemy is induced to surrender rather than fight a battle with the subsequent loss of life. The moral problem in applying 'just war' theory thus lies not with the use of fear as a weapon, but in the choice of possible targets.

Terrorism as a policy has had a long history. One of the earliest examples in fact comes from first-century Palestine, the 'sicarii' active in the Zealot struggle during and after the fall of Jerusalem (AD 66–73). Their favourite weapon was a short sword, a 'sica', with which they struck at people in crowds. They also used sabotage, burning the public archives and damaging the city's water supply. However, as Walter Laqueur points out, our own century has witnessed an unparalleled savagery in the methods employed:

> Standards and modes of behaviour have changed. The Narodnaya Volya [the Russian movement respon- sible for the assassination of Czar Alexander II in 1881], the French Anarchists or the Irish dynamiters would not have abducted children and threatened to kill them unless ransom was paid, they would not have hired agents to do their own work, nor would they have given parcels with explosives to unsuspect- ing tourists. (*Terrorism*, pp. 162–3)

Why there has been this change, it is difficult to say for certain. My own suspicion is that it is due to the dominance of the two secular moralities to which we referred in the first chapter, Utilitarianism and Marxism. For both urge that only the total good be taken into account, and on that scenario any innocent people who are harmed in the process become mere statistics in the total calculation. At any rate, it would help to explain why the apparent ideal- ism of groups like the Italian Red Brigade or the German Baader-Meinhoff can be so easily harnessed into such callous disregard for the value of individual human life. But it is possible that the explanation is more prosaic. For another difference is that the modern terrorist is never short of money. There are always governments willing to lend either out of sympathy for the cause or more commonly simply to embarrass other governments. Thus, according to figures given in Laqueur, in 1975 Fatah had a budget of

150—200 million dollars and even the IRA had 1—3 million dollars. The explanation may then simply be that in the past terrorists were forced to concentrate their energies on the guilty, whereas there are now sufficient funds to enable them to range as widely as they like.

Whatever the explanation, what needs emphasizing is that the heartless immorality of most modern terrorism does not prove that there could not in practice be a terrorist campaign waged according to the principles of 'the just war'. It would mean intending to strike only at the guilty, surely by no means an impossible self-limitation. Indeed, one might even argue that it would be a better world if more Christians were prepared to contemplate support for terrorist movements in situations of acute injustice. For, if they were then in positions of influence with the guerillas, there might be more hope of there being the discrimination in the campaign that Christianity demands.

Torture is in part a response to terrorism, but it certainly cannot be explained wholly in those terms. Its practice is far too arbitrary for that. Any kind of opposition, including passive resistance, may be dealt with in this kind of way. It also is one of the great scourges of this century, though Amnesty International has done much valuable work in attempting to contain it. The work of this protest organization, founded in 1961 by a Roman Catholic lawyer, Peter Benenson, is movingly told in Jonathan Power's recent account, *Against Oblivion*. However, despite the faith of its founder, there will be those who point to Christianity's own use of torture to suggest that its present opposition is pure expediency. On the contrary, what I want to suggest is that its introduction and use by the Inquisition was perhaps the darkest period in the history of Christian moral thought, and that this provides a salutary warning of what may happen again if Christianity ever abandons that most basic Gospel insight of all, Christ's teaching and example of love with its emphasis on the sacredness and unique value of each and every human being.

157

The Church's record on torture, apart from one passing and reluctant concession by Augustine in *The City of God*, was in fact perfect until 1252. Numerous condemnations are to be found. Typical is the emphatic verdict of the ninth-century pope, Nicholas I, who in a letter to Prince Boris of Bulgaria declares that 'it is a thing that neither divine law nor human can admit'. Yet all this changed with Innocent IV's bull, *Ad Extirpanda*, allowing captured heretics to be tortured. It would be nice if one could claim that the motive was the laudable one of trying to save the heretic's soul from damnation. That this was sometimes so is admitted by H. C. Lea, author of the standard history, *The Inquisition in the Middle Ages*. But there is no such hint in the bull, and the real explanation unfortunately lies elsewhere. As Walter Ullmann suggests in his introduction to this book, it was a product of medieval collectivist thinking. 'Society was one whole, was indivisible, was one totum and the individual was no more than a part of the whole. What mattered was the well-being of society, and not of the parts constituting it.'

That the Church has a social side, the emphasis on the building of the divine society, we have already noted. But it is an emphasis that must never be allowed to override the sacredness of the person, as torture does — physically and psychologically destroying him for the alleged good of society. Love binds together the whole, without destroying its parts.

FURTHER READING

On pacifism and self-defence

Leo Tolstoy, *On Civil Disobedience and Non-violence*, Mentor Books, New York, 1967

Jean-Michel Hornus, *It Is Not Lawful for Me to Fight*, Herald Press, Pennsylvania and Paternoster Press, Exeter, 1980

On the 'just war'

Michael Walzer, *Just and Unjust Wars*, Penguin, 1980

Paul Ramsey, *War and the Christian Conscience*, Duke University Press, USA, 1961

Paul Ramsey, *The Just War*, Charles Scribner's Sons, New York, 1968

On nuclear war

Walter Stein (ed.), *Nuclear Weapons: A Catholic Response*, Burns & Oates, 1963 (recently reissued)

Solly Zuckerman, *Nuclear Illusion and Reality*, Collins, 1982

On conflict within the state

Walter Laqueur, *Terrorism*, Abacus/Sphere Books, 1978

Jonathan Power, *Against Oblivion*, Fontana, 1981

References

For a guide to reading on a particular topic, see the list at the end of the relevant chapter.

Antoninus, St, *Summa Theologica Moralis*, 4 vols, Verona, 1740
Aquinas, St Thomas, *Summa Theologiae*, Blackfriars edn, Eyre & Spottiswoode, 1963, see esp. vols 16, 23, 28, 34, 35, 38
Aristotle, *Politics*, Penguin, 1962
Assman, H., *Practical Theology of Liberation*, Search Press, 1975
Atkinson, D., *To Have and to Hold*, Collins, 1975
Augustine, St *The City of God*, Penguin, 1972
Boesak, A. A., *Black Theology: Black Power*, A. R. Mowbray, 1978
Bonino, J., *Revolutionary Theology comes of Age*, SPCK, 1975
Boswell, J., *Christianity, Social Tolerance and Homosexuality*, University of Chicago Press, 1980
Bradford School of Peace Studies (see Rogers, *et al.*)
Brandt report, *North—South: A Programme for Survival*, Pan Books, 1980
Brody, B., *Abortion and the Sanctity of Human Life*, MIT Press, 1976
Brown, J. A. C., *The Social Psychology of Industry*, Penguin, 1954
Brown, P., *Augustine of Hippo*, Faber & Faber, 1967
Butler, J., *Fifteen Sermons Preached at the Rolls Chapel* (ed. T. A. Roberts), SPCK, 1970
Calvin, J., *Institutes of the Christian Religion* (Library of Christian Classics, vol. XX), Westminster Press, Philadelphia, 1960
Camara, H., *Church and Colonialism*, Sheed & Ward, 1969
Catoir, J. T., *Catholics and Broken Marriage*, Ave Maria Press, Indiana, 1979
Church of England report, *Homosexual Relationships*, Church Information Office, London, 1979
Clegg, H. A., *The Changing System of Industrial Relations in Great Britain*, Blackwell, 1979

Cone, J., *A Black Theology of Liberation*, Lippincott, Philadelphia, 1970

Cone, J., *God of the Oppressed*, SPCK, 1977

Curran, C. (ed.), *Absolutes in Moral Theology*, Greenwood Press, Westport, 1975

Dahrendorf, R., *Society and Democracy in Germany*, Weidenfeld & Nicolson, 1968

Dante, A., *The Divine Comedy*, (trans. J. D. Sinclair), Oxford University Press, 1961

Demant, V. A., *Religion and the Decline of Capitalism* (Holland Lectures 1949), Faber & Faber, 1952

Devine, P., *The Ethics of Homicide*, Cornell University Press, 1978

Dominian, J., *Marriage, Faith and Love*, Darton, Longman & Todd, 1981

Euthanasia and Clinical Practice, Linacre Centre, London, 1982

Farrer, A., *Saving Belief*, Hodder & Stoughton, 1964

Fierro, A., *The Militant Gospel*, SCM, 1977

Fletcher, J., *Humanhood: Essays in Biomedical Ethics*, Prometheus Books, Buffalo, 1979

Fletcher, J., *Situation Ethics*, SCM, 1966

Fogarty, M., *The Just Wage*, G. Chapman, 1961

Furlong, M., *Divorce: One Woman's View*, Mother's Union, London, 1981

Furnish, V. P., *The Love Command in the New Testament*, SCM, 1973

Glover, J., *Causing Death and Saving Lives*, Penguin, 1977

Goergen, D., *The Sexual Celibate*, Seabury Press, New York, 1974

Goldthorpe, J., *The Affluent Worker*, Cambridge University Press, 1971

Gutierrez, G., *A Theology of Liberation*, SCM, 1974

Hackett, J., *The Third World War, August 1985*, Sidgwick & Jackson, 1978

Hare, R., *Moral Thinking*, Oxford University Press, 1981

Häring, B., *Medical Ethics*, St Paul Publications, Slough, 1974

Häring, B., *Moral Theology for Priests and Laity*, St Paul Publications, Slough, 1978

Herzberg, F., *Work and the Nature of Man*, Staples Press, 1968

Hornus, J-M., *It Is Not Lawful for Me to Fight*, Paternoster Press, Exeter, 1980

Hyman, R., *Strikes*, Fontana/Collins, 1977

Illich, I., *Limits to Medicine*, Penguin, 1977

Jaques, E., *Equitable Payment*, Heinemann, 1970

John XXIII, *Mater et Magistra*, Catholic Truth Society, 1961

John Paul II, *Laborem Exercens*, Catholic Truth Society, 1981

Joyce, J. A., *The War Machine*, Hamlyn, 1981

Keble, J., *Letters of Spiritual Counsel and Guidance*, 5th edn, J. H. Parker, Oxford, 1885

Kennedy, I., *The Unmasking of Medicine*, Allen & Unwin, 1981

Kenny, A., 'Postscript: Counterforce and Countervalue', in *Nuclear Weapons: A Catholic Response* (ed. W. Stein)

Kluge, E., *The Practice of Death*, Yale University Press, 1975

Kosnick, A. (ed.), *Human Sexuality: New Directions in Catholic Thought*, Search Press, 1977

Lane, T. and Roberts, K., *Strike at Pilkingtons*, Fontana, 1981

Laqueur, W., *Terrorism*, Abacus/Sphere Books, 1978

Lea, H., *The Inquisition in the Middle Ages*, Eyre & Spottiswoode, 1963

Leo XIII, *Rerum Novarum*, Catholic Truth Society, 1891

McAdoo, H. R., *The Structure of Caroline Moral Theology*, Longman, 1949

MacFarlane, L. J., *The Right to Strike*, Penguin, 1981

Mackie, J., *Ethics*, Penguin, 1977

McNeill, J. J., *The Church and the Homosexual*, Darton, Longman & Todd, 1977

Marx, K. and Engels, F., *Communist Manifesto*, in *Marx and Engels: Basic Writings* (ed. L. W. Feuer), Penguin, 1969

Maurice, F. D., *The Kingdom of Christ* (1838), 2 vols (ed. A. R. Vidler), SCM, 1958

Maurice, F. D., *Theological Essays*, J. Clarke, 1957

Mayhew, P., *Justice in Industry*, SCM, 1980

Meyendorff, J., *Marriage: an Orthodox Perspective*, St Vladimir's Seminary Press, 1975

Mill, J. S., *Utilitarianism* (ed. M. Warnock), Fontana/Collins, 1962

Miranda, J., *Marx and the Bible*, SCM, 1977

Newman, J. H., *Difficulties of Anglicans*, vol. 1, Longmans, Green & Co., 1897

Newman, J. H., *Parochial and Plain Sermons*, vol. II, Rivingtons, 1868

Newman, J. H., *University Sermons* (ed. D. M. Mackinnon and J. D. Holmes), SPCK, 1970

Newman, J. H., *'Via Media'*, vol. I: *Lectures on the Prophetic Office of the Church*, Longmans, Green & Co., 1891

Norman, E., *Christianity and the World Order*, Oxford University Press, 1979

Origen, *Contra Celsum* (trans. H. Chadwick), Cambridge University Press, 1953

Packard, V., *The Hidden Persuaders*, 2nd edn, Penguin, 1981

Paskins, B. and Dockrill, M., *The Ethics of War*, Duckworth, 1979

Paul VI, *Humanae Vitae*, Catholic Truth Society, 1968

Peck, W. G., *The Social Implications of the Oxford Movement*, C. Scribner's Sons, New York, 1933

Peschke, C., *Christian Ethics*, 2 vols, Goodliffe Neale, Dublin, 1979

Phelps Brown, H., *The Inequality of Pay*, Oxford University Press, 1979

Pius XI, *Quadragesimo Anno*, Catholic Truth Society, 1931

Power, J., *Against Oblivion*, Fontana/Collins, 1981

Preston, R. H. (ed.), *Industrial Conflicts and their Place in Modern Society*, SCM, 1974

Preston, R. H. (ed.), *Perspectives on Strikes*, SCM, 1975

Pusey, E. B., *Nine Sermons Preached before the University of Oxford*, Innes & Co., 1891

Rachels, J., 'Active and Passive Euthanasia', in *Killing and Let Die* (ed. B. Steinbock)

Ramsey, P., *Basic Christian Ethics*, University of Chicago Press, 1980

Ramsey, P., *The Just War*, C. Scribner's Sons, New York, 1968

Ramsey, P., *War and the Christian Conscience*, Duke University Press, 1961

Robinson, J., *Honest to God*, SCM, 1963

Rogers, P. *et al.*, *As Lambs to the Slaughter*, Arrow Books, 1981

Russell, F., *The Just War in the Middle Ages*, Cambridge University Press, 1977

Scanzoni, L. and Mollenkott, V. R., *Is the Homosexual my Neighbour?*, SCM, 1978

Schillebeeckx, E., *Marriage: Human Reality and Saving Mystery*, Sheed & Ward, 1976

Schumacher, E. F., *Small is Beautiful*, Abacus/Sphere Books, 1974

Segundo, J. L., *The Liberation of Theology*, Gill & Macmillan, Dublin, 1977

Smith, D., 'On Letting Some Babies Die', in *Killing and Let Die*, (ed. B. Steinbock)

Sobrino, J., *Christology at the Crossroads*, SCM, 1978

Stein, W. (ed.), *Nuclear Weapons: A Catholic Response*, Burns & Oates, 1963

Steinbock, B. (ed.), *Killing and Let Die*, Prentice-Hall, 1980

Storr, A., *Sexual Deviation*, Penguin, 1964

Sumner, L. W., *Abortion and Moral Theory*, Princeton University Press, 1981

Tawney, R. H., *Religion and the Rise of Capitalism* (1926), Penguin, 1969

Taylor, M., 'Evaluating Strikes', in *Perspectives on Strikes* (ed. R. H. Preston), SCM, 1975

Thielicke, H., *Theological Ethics*, 3 vols, Eerdmans, Grand Rapids, Michigan, 1979, esp. vol. 1: *Foundations* and vol. 2: *Politics*

Thompson, E. P. (ed.), *Protest and Survive*, Penguin, 1980

Tolstoy, L., *On Civil Disobedience and Non-Violence*, Mentor Books, New York, 1967

Trotsky, L., Dewey, J. and Novack, G., *Their Morals and Ours*, Pathfinder Press, New York, 1973

Van Der Marck, W., *Love and Fertility*, Sheed & Ward, 1965

Walzer, M., *Just and Unjust Wars*, Penguin, 1980

Ward, W. G., *The Ideal of a Christian Church*, 2nd edn, James Toovey, 1844

Wesley, J., 'Circumcision of the Heart', in *Sermons on Several Occasions* J. Bumpus, London, 1823

Whyte, W., *The Organisation Man*, Penguin, 1960

Williams, B. (ed.), *Obscenity and Film Censorship*, HMSO, 1979, (abridged edn, Cambridge University Press, 1981)

Williams, I., *On Reserve in Communicating Religious Knowledge* (Tract 80), in *Tracts for the Times*, vol. IV, J. H. Parker, Oxford, 1839

Woods, T., *English Casuistical Divinity*, SPCK, 1952

Zuckerman, S., *Nuclear Illusion and Reality*, Collins, 1982

Index